Robotics

DISCOVER THE SCIENCE AND TECHNOLOGY OF THE FUTURE

WITH **20** PROJECTS

KATHY CECERI

Illustrated by Sam Carbaugh

~ Upcoming Titles in the *Build It Yourself* Series ~

Visit **nomadpress.net** for a complete listing of Nomad Press titles.

 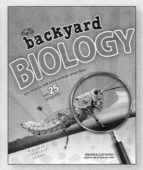  

Nomad Press
A division of Nomad Communications
10 9 8 7 6 5 4 3 2 1

This book was manufactured by Sheridan Books,
Ann Arbor, MI USA.
August 2012, Job# 338683
ISBN: 978-1-93674-976-8

Illustrations by Samuel Carbaugh
Educational Consultant Marla Conn

Questions regarding the ordering of this book should be addressed to
Independent Publishers Group
814 N. Franklin St.
Chicago, IL 60610
www.ipgbook.com

Nomad Press
2456 Christian St.
White River Junction, VT 05001
www.nomadpress.net

Contents

Timeline: The History of Robots and Robotics

200 BCE	Mechanical musical group presented to Chinese emperor.
1464 CE	Italian artist and inventor Leonardo da Vinci designs a mechanical knight at age 12.
1801	French silk cloth maker Joseph Marie Jacquard builds a machine that weaves different patterns automatically.
1822	English mathematician Charles Babbage uses Jacquard's idea to create a mechanical calculator called the Analytical Engine.
1842	English writer Ada Lovelace designs an early computer program for Babbage's invention.
1898	Serbian-American inventor Nikola Tesla demonstrates the world's first remote-control device in New York City.
1921	Czech writer Karel Capek invents the word "robot" in his play R.U.R.
1941	American science fiction writer Isaac Asimov invents the word "robotics" in his book I, Robot.
1947	The invention of the transistor makes small, light, movable computers and robots possible.
1958	Cheap, compact microprocessors make it possible to add computing ability to almost any kind of electric device.
1961	Unimate, the first robot used in a factory, is installed in a General Motors automobile plant in New Jersey.
1966	Joseph Weizenbaum of MIT designs Eliza, the earliest chatbot that can hold a conversation like a person.
1967	Mathematician Seymour Papert of the MIT Artificial Intelligence Laboratory develops the Logo language for students to program a turtle robot.
1986	Honda begins work on a walking robot, the first ASIMO.
1989	Robotics physicist Mark W. Tilden invents simple but lifelike solar-powered BEAM robots.
1989	World Chess Champion Garry Kasparov wins against a chess-playing IBM computer called Deep Thought.

1992	FIRST Robotics Competition for students, founded by inventor Dean Kamen, holds its first season.
1997	The IBM chess-playing robot Deep Blue wins against Garry Kasparov.
1998	Cynthia Breazeal of the MIT Media Lab Personal Robots Group produces Kismet, a robotic face that can show feelings.
1998	LEGO releases its MindStorms Robotic Invention System, developed with MIT.
1999	Intuitive Surgical introduces the da Vinci Surgical System, which helps doctors operate using miniature medical tools.
2001	The Talon military robot is used by rescue workers after the September 11 attack on the World Trade Center.
2002	The first popular home robot, the Roomba vacuum cleaner, is sold by iRobot.
2004	The NASA robot rovers Spirit and Opportunity begin exploration of Mars.
2004	Robosapien, a humanoid toy robot invented by Mark Tilden, is released by WowWee.
2008	A study by Saint Louis University finds that Aibo, a robotic dog made by Sony, is just as good at cheering up residents at a home for the elderly as a live dog.
2010	On roads in California, the Internet search company Google tests a self-driving car developed by computer scientist Sebastian Thrun of Stanford University.
2011	After a massive earthquake in Japan, iRobot PackBots are sent in to investigate a flood-damaged nuclear power plant.
2011	A Girl Scout team wins $20,000 for a robotic hand called the BOB-1 in the First LEGO League competition.
2011	The IBM computer Watson beats two top human players on the TV game show Jeopardy.
2012	Hospitals in the United States begin using the ReWalk-powered exoskeleton with paralyzed patients.

THE WORLD OF ROBOTICS

Welcome to the amazing world of robots! Remember the robots from movies like *Star Wars* and *Wall-E*? Not that long ago, robots were only found in science fiction. Today, real robots are everywhere!

Words to Know

robot: a machine that is able to sense, think, and act on its own.

robotics: the science of designing, building, controlling, and operating robots.

technology: scientific or mechanical tools and methods used to do something.

engineering: the use of science and math in the design and construction of things.

science fiction: a story set in the future about contact with other worlds and imaginary science and technology.

humanoid: looking like a human being.

Robots can do many different kinds of jobs, like assembling massive cars and tiny computer chips. They help doctors perform delicate surgery. Maybe you have a robot that vacuums your house or mows your lawn. In war zones, robots hunt for hidden bombs. We send robots to explore the depths of the ocean and the expanse of space.

But robots don't just do dangerous, tricky, or boring work for us. Robot toys play with us, follow our commands, and respond to our moods. Experimental robot pets keep people company in nursing homes. Musical robots accompany popular musicians.

Robotics is the science of designing, building, controlling, and operating robots.

FUN FACTS

The word "robotics" was first used in a short story in 1941. In *I, Robot*, **science fiction** writer Isaac Asimov describes **humanoid** robots built to work on Earth and in outer space. It was made into a movie starring Will Smith in 2004.

Creating a robot requires knowledge in STEM. This is science, **technology**, **engineering**, and math. But it takes experts in many different areas to create robots. They include scientists who study plants and animals and the way people think and behave, as well as inventors, builders, designers, and artists.

Robotics is also a popular hobby. Kids and adults enjoy making their own robots from kits, or from parts they find themselves. Lots of interesting robot designs have been built by robotics fans working in their own homes or with other people in robotics clubs.

Words to Know

electronics: devices that use computer parts to control the flow of electricity.

scavenged: saved from something that is broken or no longer used.

Robots may be machines, but for many people the goal is to build robots that act as if they're alive. Maybe one day we'll have robots that seem almost as human as we are.

Make Your Own Robots

The activities in *Robotics: Discover the Science and Technology of the Future,* will let you use your skills and imagination to come up with creative solutions to tricky problems. Robotics is a great way to experiment with **electronics**. Best of all, when you're done you'll have some cool robot models that really work!

Most of the activities in this book require no special equipment or tools. You can use ordinary craft materials and **scavenged** parts.

3

Where to Find Parts

It's easy to find parts to build simple, do-it-yourself robot models without spending a lot of money.

- **Recycled toys and household devices:** Many old items you may find at home, garage sales, or thrift shops have motors, switches, wiring, batteries, LED lightbulbs, tubing, and pumps that you can reuse.

Safety First!

Please make sure you ask permission before taking anything apart, and get an adult to help you with anything hard to open. If you are taking something apart that has an electric cord, first make sure it is unplugged. Then have an adult cut the cord off and throw it away!

Ed Sobey's book *Unscrewed* has lots of ideas and instructions for finding useful parts in recycled devices such as water guns and remote-controlled toys. Here are some safety tips from his book:

- Wear eye protection. Safety goggles can be found at hardware and dollar stores.

- Before you break something open, see if you can figure out how it was put together and then take it apart the same way.

- If you need to pry something open, push away from yourself.

- When taking apart electrical devices like cameras, watch out for ***capacitors***. Capacitors look like small barrels or batteries with two wire "legs." They are used to store electricity and may give you a powerful shock if you touch the wires. To make them safe, hold on to a screwdriver by the wooden or plastic handle ONLY. Then tap the metal end of the screwdriver on both "legs" of the capacitor at the same time. If there's a charge, you'll see a little spark as it discharges. Do this a few times until no more sparks appear.

Words to Know

capacitor: an electrical component (like a battery) that stores an electrical charge and releases it all at once when needed.

Look for wooden, metal, or plastic building sets, such as Tinker Toys, Erector Sets, and LEGOs. Try old remote-controlled cars and computer parts like a mouse or keyboard. Use old dolls, cans, tins, boxes, toy cars, and CDs for robot bodies, wheels, arms, and legs. Greeting cards that play music have tiny speakers you can use.

• **Household and craft materials:** Cardboard, wood, aluminum foil, and glue can be used to make robot bodies and electrical circuits. You can add personality to your robots with paint, string, googly

eyes, pipe cleaners, and other decorations. Craft stores also sell doll parts (arms, legs, eyes), foam core boards, craft foam sheets, and other useful supplies.

• **Dollar and discount stores:** Look for small, cheap, hand-held electric fans, electric toothbrushes, radios, keychain lights, calculators, or solar garden lights that are easy to take apart.

• **Electronics and hobby stores:** New supplies such as solar panels, servo motors, switches, wire, and batteries.

• **Robotics, science, and electronics surplus supply web sites:** Look online for robot kits, circuit boards, and microcontrollers.

What Is a Robot, Exactly?

Before you start working on your own robot models, let's learn what makes a robot a robot. If you look in the dictionary, you'll find "robot" defined as a machine that looks and acts like a human being. That description might work for movie robots, but in real life robots take many forms. Household robotic vacuums look like giant hockey pucks. In a factory, a robot can be just an arm. There are robots in the shape of cars, insects, or even entire houses!

Words to Know

roboticist: a scientist who works with robots.

Sense-Think-Act Cycle: a decision-making process used by robots.

bionic: a mechanical or computer-driven device that replaces or improves the normal ability of a body part.

To most **roboticists**, a robot is a machine that can go through the **Sense-Think-Act Cycle**.

• **Sense:** to take in information about what is going on around it.

• **Think:** to use that information to select the next step to take.

• **Act:** to do something that affects the outside world.

Robotics and Bioengineering

Bioengineering is the use of science, math, and building techniques on living things. Robotic bioengineers design machines that can help people live better lives. In 2011, a team of Girl Scouts from Iowa competing in the First LEGO League robot design contest invented a **bionic** hand called the BOB-1. It was designed to be made out of moldable plastic, a pencil grip, and Velcro. Thanks to the BOB-1, a three-year-old girl named Danielle who was born without fingers was able to hold a pencil for the first time. The BOB-1 design won the top $20,000 award.

BOB-1

To complete the cycle, a robot needs to have at least three kinds of parts. A **sensor** detects what's going on. A **controller** reacts to what the sensor detects. And an **effector** can take action.

A robot can have many other parts, like a **drive system** that makes a robot move from place to place, and a body to hold the parts together. You'll learn more about the parts of a robot later in this book and get to make some simple versions of your own!

Words to Know

sensor: in robotics, a device to detect what's going on outside the machine.

controller: a switch, computer, or microcontroller that can react to what the sensor detects.

effector: a device that lets the robot affect things in the outside world, such as a gripper, tool, laser beam, or display panel.

drive system: wheels, legs, or other parts that make a robot move.

computer: a device for storing and working with information.

microcontroller: a very small device that works like a mini-computer.

Robots Without Brains

Not all roboticists agree with the "Sense-Think-Act" definition of a robot. Some believe that a robot is any machine that can act on its own. Even robots that don't have "brains" can behave in surprisingly lifelike ways. Some move around at random. Others react automatically to signals from their sensors.

More and more researchers and hobbyists are interested in these simple, behavior-based robots without **computers** or **microcontrollers**. They are cheaper and easier to build than robots with controllers. And they can be used as models to help scientists build more complicated robots.

ROBOT ... OR NOT A ROBOT?

How can you tell whether a device meets the Sense-Think-Act definition of a robot? One way is to test it by going through the steps of a *flowchart*. Flowcharts are used in designing *computer programs*. Different shaped boxes represent a type of action. An oval means "Start" or "End." A diamond-shaped Decision Block contains a question that you have to answer. Arrows show you what order to go in.

Use the flowchart on page 10 to decide whether a device meets the Sense-Think-Act definition. Test some of the devices in step 5. Follow the directions to make a list of devices you might have seen and what parts they contain. Then use that *data* to answer the questions on the flowchart.

Words to Know

flowchart: a diagram that shows the steps to go through to solve a problem.

computer program: a set of step-by-step instructions that tells a computer what to do with the information it has to work with.

data: information, usually given in the form of numbers, that can be processed by a computer.

SUPPLIES

- computer, or paper and pencil

1 On a piece of paper or your computer, make a list with four columns. Label the columns "Device," "Sensor," "Controller," and "Effector."

2 In the Device column, list common machines that might qualify as robots (see step 5 for suggestions).

3 For the first device, go to the Sensor column. Write down what kind of sensors it has. If it doesn't have any sensors, write "none." Do the same for the Controller and Effector column.

4 Continue down the list of devices, filling in the answers across each row of columns.

5 To use the flowchart, start at the oval at the top. Follow the arrows, answering the questions in the diamond-shaped Decision Blocks using the data in your list.

Suggestions for devices:

- television
- automatic garage door opener
- calculator
- clothes dryer
- automatic supermarket door
- electric toothbrush
- smoke detector
- automatic soap dispenser

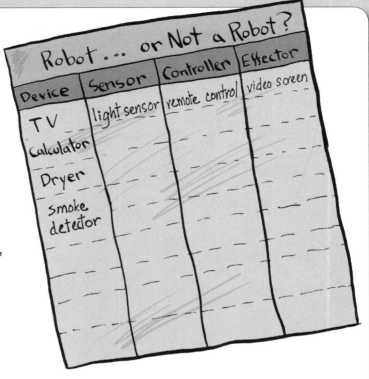

Robot . . . or Not a Robot?			
Device	Sensor	Controller	Effector
TV	light sensor	remote control	video screen
Calculator			
Dryer			
smoke detector			

SENSE — THINK — ACT

continues on next page . . .

Robot . . . or Not a Robot Flowchart

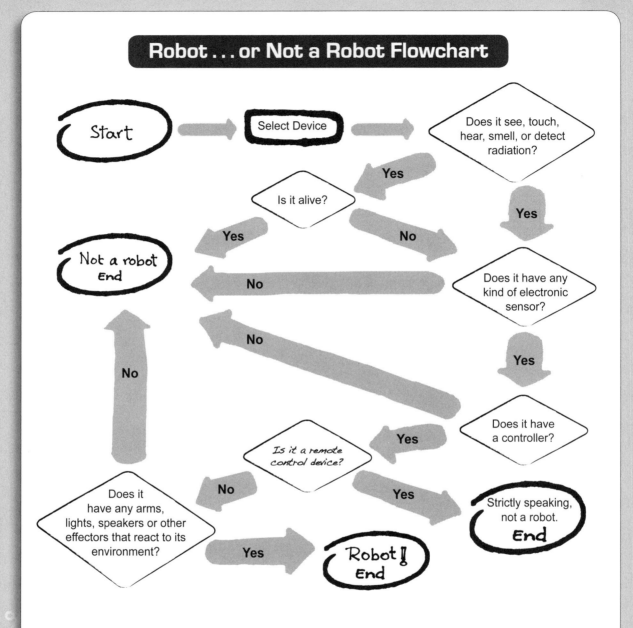

Answers to Try This: Robot . . . or Not a Robot?

Television (TV): light sensor (remote control), video screen; **automatic garage door opener:** touch sensor or motion sensor (remote control), remote control, door opener; **calculator:** keyboard (touch sensor), microcontroller, display screen; **clothes dryer:** temperature shut-off switch, no controller, motor; **supermarket door:** motion sensor, no controller, motor; **electric toothbrush:** on/off switch, no controller, motor; **smoke detector:** smoke sensor, no controller, alarm horn; **automatic soap dispenser:** motion sensor, no controller, motor.

DEVELOPMENT OF ROBOTICS

Robots that can sense, think, and act for themselves have only been possible since electronic computers were invented about 50 years ago. But long before that, *automata* were already entertaining and doing work for humans.

ROBOTICS

Words to Know

automata: machines that can move by themselves (singular is automaton).

loom: a machine for weaving thread into cloth.

As early as 200 BCE, a device that used air pipes and ropes pulled by hand to make mechanical musicians play flutes and stringed instruments entertained the emperor of China. Over 1,600 years later, when the famous Italian artist and inventor Leonardo da Vinci was just 12 years old, he designed a mechanical knight. Dressed in a suit of armor, the knight could sit up and move its arms and head. Then, around 1555 CE, an Italian clockmaker named Gianello Torriano, built a wind-up model of a lady that could walk around in a circle while strumming a type of guitar called a lute. You can see the *Lute Player Lady* in a museum in Vienna, Austria, today.

Soon, inventors started putting automated machines to work. A French silk weaver named Joseph Marie Jacquard built a **loom** in 1801 that automatically created patterns as it wove thread into cloth.

BCE? CE?

What does it mean when dates end with the letters BCE or CE? The beginning of the Common Era is marked by the birth of Jesus and begins with the year 1. These years are sometimes followed by the letters CE. Events that happened before the first year of the Common Era are marked as BCE, or Before the Common Era. The years BCE may seem backward, because as time passes the years actually become smaller in number. For example, a child born in 300 BCE would celebrate turning 10 in the year 290 BCE. Think of it as a countdown to the Common Era.

Words to Know

punch card: a card with holes punched in it that gives directions to a machine or computer.

radio transmitter: the part of a radio that sends signals.

feedback: information about the result of an action that is sent back to the person or machine that performed the action.

communication: sharing information with another person or machine.

Turing test: a series of questions to test whether a computer can think like a human being.

In 1822, English mathematician Charles Babbage used **punch cards** in his Analytical Engine, a mechanical calculator. His friend Lady Ada Lovelace designed a series of steps to make Babbage's engine solve certain math problems. Lovelace's work is considered the world's first computer program. And in 1898 in New York, the electrical pioneer Nikola Tesla showed off the first remote-control device: a mechanical boat controlled by a **radio transmitter**.

Research into computerized robots began after World War II. In 1948, mathematician Norbert Wiener wrote a book called *Cybernetics* that compared the way people and machines functioned. He found that people and machines both use **feedback**, **communication**, and control to make decisions and take action. In 1950, computer scientist Alan Turing came up with the **Turing test** to see whether a machine was able to think like a human. To pass the test, a computer had to fool people into thinking they were talking to a person.

FUN FACTS

The word "robot" was first used by writer Karel Capek in the play *R.U.R.* in 1921. It comes from the Czech word *robota*, which means slave labor. *R.U.R.* is about a company called Rossum´s Universal Robots that creates robot workers. It's one of the first stories in which robots rebel against their human masters and try to take over the world.

13

In 1959, the Massachusetts Institute of Technology (MIT) opened a laboratory to study artificial intelligence (AI), which is the ability of a machine to act as if it thinks like a human. MIT is still a leader in robotics research.

Robots in Fiction

Some of the best-known robots appear only in stories. In ancient Greek mythology, Hephaestus, the god of metalwork, built a giant man called Talos out of bronze to guard the island of Crete. Here are some other famous fictional robots:

• **Maria:** This metallic humanoid appeared in the silent film *Metropolis* in 1927. It was the first robot movie ever made. Maria was disguised as a real person by the bad guys, who used her to try to stop unhappy factory workers from complaining.

• **HAL 9000 Computer:** In the movie *2001: A Space Odyssey*, HAL controlled a spaceship and worked with human astronauts. His "body" was the ship itself, and he had glowing round red lights in the spaceship's walls that served as his eyes. Although he wasn't evil, HAL later broke down and tried to destroy the crew.

• **R2-D2 and C-3PO:** These helper droids from the 1977 movie *Star Wars* may be the most famous robots of all time. R2-D2 looked like a large rolling can and "talked" using only beeps and whistles. C-3PO was a golden-colored metallic man who could speak many languages. Together with Luke Skywalker and his friends, they fought the Empire and the evil Darth Vader.

• **WALL-E:** This box-like machine was the last working robot on Earth in the 2008 animated film of the same name. Everyone on the planet left aboard a giant spaceship. Only WALL-E remained to clean up the piles of garbage left behind. When a more advanced robot named EVE arrived to search for signs of life, WALL-E found love and adventure.

People build, study, and use robots today in many different ways. At home, people use robots for their everyday tasks. Government robotics researchers develop rugged robots for use in the military and in scientific exploration. Hobbyists and artists get creative with robots they build themselves from kits, parts, and salvaged equipment. And business people work with engineers to make robots less expensive and more useful so that more people and companies will buy them.

FUN FACTS

A working automaton built by Henri Maillardet around 1810 is on display at the Franklin Institute in Philadelphia. It looks like a boy in a clown's costume, and can draw and write poetry in French and English. The machine was the inspiration for the drawing automaton in the book *The Invention of Hugo Cabret* by Brian Selznick and the movie *Hugo*.

Robotics in the Home

The Roomba vacuum cleaner appeared in stores in 2002. It was the first popular home robot. Other common household robots include lawn mowers, floor washers, and swimming pool cleaners.

Words to Know

webcam: a camera attached to a computer that can send photos or video over the Internet.

Internet: a communications network that allows computers around the world to share information.

Mobile **webcams** let you see what is happening in your home or office while you are away. They can be controlled over the **Internet** with a cell phone or game console.

15

Hackbots

When the Roomba first came out, fans began **hacking** the vacuum to see if they could program it themselves. So the company came out with Create, a version designed to be hacked. Now hobbyists can program their Create robots to play laser tag, dance, and even be steered by a hamster in a ball attached to the top!

Words to Know

hacking: using electronics skills to make a device do something it was not designed to do.

smart home: a house in which all electric devices are monitored or controlled by a computer.

prototype: an experimental model.

animatronic: making a puppet or other lifelike figure move on its own with electronics.

Bill Gates, the founder of the giant computer company Microsoft, built a **smart home** near Seattle, Washington, in the 1990s. It could be programmed to turn on lights, adjust the temperature, and play his favorite music when he entered a room.

Robotics in Toys

Robotics kits and toys aren't just for kids. Adult hobbyists and researchers use them to build robotic **prototypes** quickly and easily. One of the first programmable robotics kits was the LEGO Mindstorms Robotic Invention System. The Mindstorms system uses a simple computer program developed at MIT. Robots are built using LEGO bricks, so no tools or wiring are required. Today robotics kits like LEGO Mindstorms and VEX, which use metallic parts that screw together, are also used by students in robotics competitions.

Many interactive toys also qualify as "real" robots. Some are **animatronic** dolls like Furby, Robosapien, or Elmo Live, which respond to touch or remote control. Others, like Hexbug robotic insects, have sensors that help them move on their own. They were created in 2007 by Innovation First, which makes the Vex Robotics Design System. There's a fast-moving Ant with rotating legs and bump sensors that make it reverse direction. The Larva uses infrared sensing to crawl around objects in its path. The zippy little Hexbug Nano has no sensors, but hackers have added their own. One hack uses a photoresistor to make the Nano scurry away from light like a cockroach.

Robotics in Art

Artists use robots to create art, and as works of art themselves. The Jackoon Artbot by Oscar D. Torres is a little robotic arm on wheels. It scoots around a sheet of paper, dipping a brush into a cup of paint and dabbing it on the paper. An art piece called "Nervous" by Bjoern Schuelke, looked like just a dangling fluffy orange ball. But the fluff ball would jump, shake, and beep when someone come near it. Inside was a **theremin**, an electronic musical instrument that responds to people coming near it.

Words to Know

theremin: an electronic musical instrument that plays different notes when you move your hands around it without touching it.

Musicians use robots too. The League of Electronic Musical Urban Robots (LEMUR) builds self-playing instruments. Their pieces feature robotic guitars, bells, gongs, and instruments made out of kitchen tools and hardware. LEMUR's robotic instruments can respond to what they hear, which allows them to play with live musicians, including the popular band They Might Be Giants.

Smart Clothing

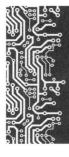

The LilyPad Arduino, developed by Leah Buechley of the MIT Media Lab, is a programmable device that can be sewn into clothing. Fashion designer Shannon Henry used it to make her Skirt Full of Stars. The Lilypad makes different colored lights flash when a sensor shows the skirt is in motion.

Robotics in Medicine

In hospitals, robots do everything from run errands to help doctors perform advanced operations. The HelpMate looks like a rolling storage cabinet. It can be programmed to deliver drugs, meals, medical records, and X-rays. It can even take the elevator by itself!

In the operating room, the da Vinci Surgical System helps doctors work with miniature tools. The doctor watches a 3D video magnifier screen and moves the controls. The robot copies each movement of the doctor's hands with its four mechanical arms.

Words to Know

cochlear implant: an electronic device that is attached to nerves under the skin to help a deaf person detect sounds.

Systems like the da Vinci let doctors make smaller cuts than would normally be possible, so the patient can heal more quickly.

Robotic medical devices also help people in their daily lives. Australian scientist Graeme Clark invented the **cochlear implant** to help deaf people detect sound. It is inserted under the skin, and sends sounds directly to the person's brain. Since 1978 almost 200,000 deaf children and adults have had cochlear implant surgery.

Words to Know

powered exoskeleton: a "robot suit" that can be worn to give a person added strength.

industrial: used in a factory, or designed to be used under hard work conditions.

Wheelchair-user Amit Goffer of Argo Medical Technologies in Israel developed the ReWalk, a **powered exoskeleton** that helps paralyzed people stand up and walk. Using motorized braces that are strapped onto the user's legs, the ReWalk moves when the person leans forward or back.

Robotics in Industry

Automobile factories and other businesses use robots to do all kinds of dirty, dangerous, boring, or difficult jobs that human workers can't do, or don't want to do. The first **industrial** robot, Unimate, was only a robotic arm. It worked in a General Motors automobile plant in New Jersey in 1961.

Many robotic features can be found in cars today. In 2006, Lexus came out with an Advanced Parking Guidance System that lets the car park itself. Sensors on the wheels use sound waves to tell the car's computer how much space it has.

The **2010 Toyota Prius** is a hybrid car with computers that switch the motor from gas to electrical power. It also has a self-parking feature.

19

Words to Know

weld: to connect metal parts by heating them until they soften.

plasma torch: a tool that uses streams of electrified gas to cut through sheets of metal.

assembly line: a way of putting together products in a factory by passing materials from one machine or person to another to do the next step.

clean room: a room in a laboratory or factory where objects that must be kept free of dust or dirt are made.

Unmanned Aerial Vehicles (UAVs): planes and other aircraft that can fly without a pilot in control.

autonomous: a robot that can plan its movements and move without human help.

Unimate could move heavy car parts and **weld** them together. Robotic arms also use **plasma torches** to cut through sheets of metal. "Pick and place" robots take materials from one spot on an **assembly line** and move them somewhere else. Unlike people, they can work long hours without getting tired. Robots are also used in factories that make delicate computer parts because they don't carry dirt or dust into the building's **clean room**.

Robotics in the Military

Planes and other aircraft that can be flown by remote control or on their own are called **Unmanned Aerial Vehicles (UAVs)**. Predator spy planes are controlled by pilots halfway around the world, using joysticks and computer screens. Mini-UAVs are small enough to fit in a Marine's backpack.

The Dragon Eye is an **autonomous** spy plane that can be launched by hand or with an elastic bungee cord.

The Amazing Dean Kamen

Dean Kamen is famous for inventing the Segway, a two-wheeled motorized scooter that balances electronically. He is also known as the founder of the FIRST robotics competition for students. But most of Kamen's inventions are designed to help people with medical problems. In 1976, he began making robotic **syringes** that patients can wear. The devices automatically give them shots of drugs whenever needed. An experimental project called the iBOT was a robotic wheelchair that could roll up and down stairs. In 2007, the Defense Advanced Research Projects Agency, or DARPA, asked Kamen to design a robotic arm to help **amputees** injured in wars. DARPA sponsors robot research for military purposes. Kamen's design became the basis of a project to build an arm that can be controlled by the user's brain. If all goes well, the arm could be available by 2015.

The military also uses many types of **portable** remote-control robots on the ground. Some look like miniature tanks and can fire machine guns or less harmful weapons like bean bags, smoke, and pepper spray. One robot, the TALON, can climb stairs, go over rock piles and barbed wire, plow through snow, and even travel short distances underwater. Its sensors can detect explosives, poisonous gas, radiation, and weapons.

The military uses robots like the TALON to defuse bombs and check dangerous areas for hazards. It was also used by rescue workers when New York's World Trade Center buildings collapsed in 2001.

Words to Know

syringe: a medical instrument used to inject fluid into the body or take fluid out.

amputee: a person who is missing an arm or leg.

portable: easily moved around.

21

ROBOTICS

Robotics in Earth Exploration

Scientists use robots to explore regions where people can't go. But it's dangerous work, even for a robot. In 1993, researchers from Carnegie Mellon University accidentally dropped an 8-legged robot called Dante into a volcano in Antarctica. The next year, they had more luck exploring a volcano in Alaska with Dante II.

That robot sent back readings from the volcano before it also disappeared down the crater.

An underwater robot called ABE helped scientists at the Woods Hole Oceanographic Institution to observe the ocean's depths from 1996 until 2010, when it was lost at sea. ABE could dive down more than 14,000 feet (4,500 meters) without having to be connected to a ship or submarine. That meant ABE could work faster, cheaper, and in more places than other research tools. ABE helped locate, map, and photograph many deep-sea hydrothermal vent sites and volcanoes. It also took magnetic readings that helped scientists understand how the earth's crust was formed. Woods Hole scientists now use a robot called Sentry, which can go even faster and deeper than ABE.

Robotics in Space

Robots and outer space have always gone together. In 1997, NASA sent the robotic rover *Sojourner* to Mars on the Pathfinder Mission. The solar-powered robot sent back pictures and analyzed the chemistry of Martian rocks and soil.

The NASA robot rovers *Spirit* and *Opportunity* landed on Mars in 2004. Although they were only expected to last 90 days, *Spirit* lasted until 2010. As of 2012, *Opportunity* was still going strong, and a new rover, *Curiosity*, was on its way to join it on the Martian surface.

Robots also serve on the International Space Station in orbit around Earth. In 2001, a robotic arm built by the Canadian Space Agency was installed. The Canadarm2 is used to handle large objects, help visiting space vehicles to dock on the station, and help astronauts with repairs and experiments outside the ship. Its pieces can be taken apart and replaced like LEGOs!

Robonaut 2 (R2), the first humanoid robot in space, was activated on the space station in 2011. Developed by NASA and car-maker General Motors, R2 consists of a head, body, and two arms. It can sit on a non-moving base or be attached to wheels, legs, or a rover, depending on its mission. Roboticists hope R2 can also be used in General Motors manufacturing plants on Earth.

FUN FACTS

The Mars rover *Spirit* made its greatest discovery because of a broken wheel. In 2007, *Spirit*'s broken wheel scraped up some bright white soil. It was made up of a mineral called silica left behind by water in the form of hot springs or steam. To scientists, this is evidence that life could be possible on Mars.

23

ART-MAKING VIBROBOT

A **vibrobot** isn't a real robot, but it acts like one. A vibrobot moves by vibrating, shaking, or jiggling along. When it touches a wall, it turns and keeps on going. But a vibrobot doesn't have a sensor or a controller to tell it what to do—it just vibrates away! A motor spins a weight to make the vibrobot vibrate. By placing the weight a little off-center, the whole vibrobot will be thrown around enough to move.

Your Art-Making Vibrobot will skitter across a piece of paper, drawing as it goes. **If you choose to use a hot glue gun, have an adult supervise.**

Words to Know

vibrobot: a robot-like toy that moves using a vibrating motor.

SUPPLIES

- small DC motor (1.5 volts)
- insulated electrical wire, about 1 foot long (30 centimeters)
- wire cutter
- electrical tape
- 1 paper, plastic, or foam cup
- foam mounting tape
- 2 AAA batteries
- rubber band
- cork
- 3 markers
- cardboard box lid or box with low-cut sides, about the size of a piece of printer paper
- plain white or light-colored paper
- *optional*: pipe cleaners, craft sticks, Styrofoam or wooden pieces, decorative glue-ons, googly eyes, glitter pens, quick-dry glue, or hot glue gun

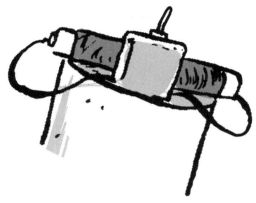

1 If your motor doesn't have wires attached, use the wire cutter to cut two pieces of wire about 6 inches long (15 centimeters). Remove about ½ inch of insulation from each end so that the metal inside is exposed (1 centimeter). Attach one wire to each of the metal terminals coming out of the motor so that metal touches metal. Secure with electrical tape. Test the motor by touching the other end of the wires to the ends of a battery. If you have a good connection, the shaft of the motor will start to turn.

2 Turn the cup upside down. Attach the motor to the bottom of the cup with the foam tape so that the wires stick out either side and the motor shaft is sticking up.

3 Line up the batteries so that the top (positive end) of one touches the bottom (negative end) of the other. Secure them together with electrical tape.

4 Put the rubber band around both batteries so that it covers the ends. Wrap more tape around to secure, if needed. Use the foam tape to secure the batteries next to (alongside) the motor.

5 Stick the end of the wires under the rubber band so that the bare wire touches the ends of the batteries. The motor shaft should turn. If not, move the wires around until it does. Turn the motor on and off by taking out one of the wires. You can tape the other wire in place.

6 Make an off-balance weight that will shake the cup by sticking a cork onto the motor shaft. You can hot glue a craft stick onto the cork to make it even more off-balance.

continues on next page . . .

9 If your Vibrobot doesn't work, or you're not happy with the way it's moving, there are a few things you can try.

• Make sure the weight on the motor isn't hitting anything on the robot.

• Try shifting the legs, the weight, or the decorations to change the balance.

• If it's too heavy it may not move very well. Remove some decoration, or use a 9V battery.

7 Use the electrical tape to attach the markers as "legs" on the cup. Decorate your robot as desired.

8 To make an arena to test out your Vibrobot, cover the inside of the box lid with a piece of paper. Take the caps off the markers, place the Vibrobot inside, and start the motor. Your Art-Making Vibrobot will dance around and bounce off the walls, covering the paper with its own designs.

HOUSING: ROBOT BODIES

Robots come in every shape and size imaginable. They range from *microscopic* research bots to giant automated cranes. And they can be made out of almost any kind of material, from stretchy fabric to the toughest plastic. Many industrial, military, and exploration robots look like everyday tools or vehicles.

Words to Know

microscopic: something so small it can only be seen using a microscope.

social robot: a robot designed to talk, play, or work with humans in a lifelike way.

Robot toys and **social robots** often look like stuffed animals or friendly imaginary creatures. UAVs resemble blisteringly fast jet planes, whirring miniature helicopters, or tiny insects. A humanoid robot usually has a face, two arms, and two legs. It can look like an old-fashioned mechanical man if it's made out of metal. But if its covering is soft and squishy like skin, it can look so real, it might scare you!

Big Robots, Little Robots

Robots also vary greatly in size. Giant autonomous John Deere tractors built by Carnegie Mellon University's National Robotics Engineering Center have been used to spray orchards of orange trees. The Takenaka Corporation of Japan uses Surf Robo, a construction robot, to automatically smooth concrete floors in highrise buildings.

At the opposite extreme, nanobots are robots that are too small to see without a microscope. At the 2009 RoboCup competition, nanobots played soccer in a stadium the size of a grain of rice. Researchers are studying ways to use nanobots to do surgery within the body. They hope to be able to use them to take photos or tissue samples or even attack cancer cells.

FUN FACTS

Sprint was a flying rover designed to float around the International Space Station with a camera, taking pictures of the astronauts working outside. It was shaped like an oversized soccer ball and covered with soft padding. The padding protected the ship and the astronauts from injury as *Sprint* floated weightlessly around them in space.

A group of small robots that work together like bees in a hive is known as a **swarm**.

In 2011, a research team from Harvard University developed the Kilobot, a vibrobot about the size of a quarter. Kilobots can be programmed to work in swarms. Because each Kilobot costs less than $15 to build, researchers are using them to see how swarms of larger robots can work together to accomplish big tasks. **Modular** robots are similar to swarms. Each one is a separate moving robot that can communicate with the others. But modular robots can also connect to form a larger robot.

The modular ckBot from the ModLab at the University of Pennsylvania looks like a collection of small black building blocks. If the blocks are kicked apart, they right themselves and crawl toward each other to join up again. Robots that can rearrange themselves like real-life Transformers or repair themselves on the go would be handy on space missions and in other hard-to-reach places.

Robot Critters

When roboticists want their machines to act like living things, they borrow ideas from nature. A **biomimetic** robot is based on an animal or other life form. In 1995, MIT engineers began testing the fish-shaped RoboTuna in its underwater tank. RoboTuna may someday help in the design of autonomous mini-submarines that swim like fish.

29

Robolobster is an underwater "sniffer" robot that traces chemical odors. Joseph Ayers of Northeastern University in Massachusetts designed Robolobster in 1998 for the US Navy. The Navy wanted a robot that could crawl along the ocean floor looking for mines. BigDog is the name of a headless, metallic, four-legged biomimetic robot that looks like a real dog as it runs. It can climb over rock paths and through mud and snow.

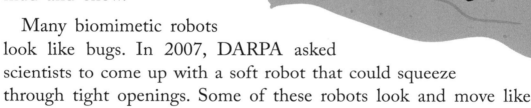

Many biomimetic robots look like bugs. In 2007, DARPA asked scientists to come up with a soft robot that could squeeze through tight openings. Some of these robots look and move like caterpillars, inchworms, or slugs.

At the University of California at Berkeley in 2008, researchers designed a tiny six-legged robot called Dash that could scamper across the floor as quickly as a cockroach.

Materials Make a Difference

Robot builders often start by making test models out of materials that are cheap and easy to work with. This way, they can make changes quickly, or build multiple versions. Wood, Styrofoam, and PVC plumbing are common materials for robot prototypes.

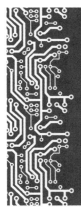

Squishy or Hard? Heavy or Light?

Robot designers have to think about a lot of things to decide which materials will work best for the machine they want to build. Will the robot need to be heavy to withstand a pounding? Or should it be as light as possible to save on the energy it needs to move? Does it have to be rigid enough to carry a heavy load? Or should it be flexible and bendy? Will the robot be working under extreme conditions and need a sturdy metal or plastic framework and covering?

Sometimes, scientists need to invent new materials for their machines. This is what they did with the soft DARPA robots. Or they might find new uses for old materials.

In order to be lightweight yet strong, the prototype for Dash, the robotic cockroach, was made out of folded cardboard. The flexible cardboard lets Dash survive long falls, even from the top of a high building.

Kids' building sets are popular for prototypes too. In 2008, student Charles Gage from the University of Bath in England used LEGO Technic bricks to build a robot crab that could crawl on land or underwater.

FUN FACTS

The Roachbot, a three-wheeled robot "driven" by a real live cockroach, won a prize in the Art & Artificial Life International Competition in Spain in 2006. The Roachbot was one of the first true half machine, half animal *cyborgs*.

Words to Know

cyborg: a human or animal that is part robot.

31

At Cornell University in New York in 1998, engineer Andy Ruina built a set of walking robot legs out of wooden Tinkertoys.

Engineer Saul Griffith of Otherlab in San Francisco, designs inflatable robots called Pneubots. They look like giant blow-up beach toys. Griffith built the first prototype out of a rubber bicycle tube for $5. Later models were made of thin fabric. They included an almost-life-sized elephant, a dinosaur, and an octopus. His six-legged Ant-Roach is a cross between an anteater and a cockroach. Ant-Roach is big and strong enough to hold two adults on its back as it walks along, but light enough for one person to carry. According to Griffith, the playful creations are really research for serious projects, such as artificial limbs or walkers. He hopes his designs will produce robots that are low cost and lightweight, yet safe and strong.

Making a robot skin that's tough, soft, and sensitive is another challenge for scientists. In 2011, at Stanford University in California, chemist Zhenan Bao demonstrated a rubbery film that can "feel." The material contains microscopic springs that stretch when pressed, even if the pressure is very light. The springs send an electrical signal to the robot's brain telling it how much pressure has been applied.

The "Uncanny Valley"

Have you ever noticed that some of the most realistic-looking robots are also the creepiest? According to scientists, there's a place between believable and not-quite-believable that gives all humans the willies. They call it the **Uncanny Valley**. When we look at a cartoon of a happy person, it makes us happy. The same thing happens with a photograph. But an almost-real robot or 3D animation? That's truly scary.

Researchers don't know why it happens, but in experiments, even monkeys that were shown pictures of almost-real monkeys turned away in fright. One idea is that being afraid of others who don't "look right" helped early humans (and monkeys) avoid catching diseases. But for companies like Hanson Robotics, it's a real problem. Artist and roboticist David Hanson makes almost-real robot heads that can talk, smile, and even make jokes. One Hanson head looks like the famous scientist Albert Einstein. The key is a special artificial skin Hanson invented called Frubber. It makes his robot faces bend and crinkle in a lifelike way. But videos of the Einstein head mounted on a shiny plastic robot body give many people the chills. The company will have to work hard to keep its fantastic machines from falling into the Uncanny Valley!

Based on the amount of pressure, the robot can detect something as light as a fly, or as heavy as an elephant. She is working on adapting the skin to absorb solar energy to power the robot and to detect other things such as chemicals or microscopic life forms in its surroundings. Some day, the robotic skin may be used to help people feel through their artificial limbs, or make computer touchscreens even more sensitive.

Words to Know

Uncanny Valley: the point at which a robot looks almost real and becomes strange and frightening.

33

SOME FRUBBERY ROBOT SKIN

Roboticists turn to chemistry when they want to create lifelike skin for humanoid robots. Here's how to mix up some Frubbery Robot Skin yourself! When you add borax to glue, a chemical change takes place that makes the glue stretchy instead of sticky. You can flatten out the mixture to make a smooth layer of Frubber-like material. Experiment with the ingredients to change the thickness, stickiness, and stretchiness. Make notes as you try different formulas, so you know which one you like best. **IMPORTANT: Be careful not to get your concoction on furniture or clothes. And don't pour it down the drain, or it will clog up your plumbing!**

1 In one plastic cup, mix the ½ cup warm water (120 milliliters) and borax. Stir until the water is cloudy.

2 In the other cup, mix the remaining water and glue. Add a drop or two of food coloring if desired. Stir until smooth.

3 Put some of the liquid from the borax cup into the glue cup. Stir for a minute and see how it changes. If the Frubbery mixture is too sticky or runny, add a little more borax mixture. You should need no more than 2 teaspoons to get a nice stretchy Frubber-like mixture (10 milliliters). When it forms a solid blob, take it out and knead it on the plate by squeezing and squishing it with your hands.

Words to Know

non-Newtonian fluid: a substance that can hold its shape like a solid and flow like a liquid.

- 2 plastic or other disposable cups
- ½ cup warm water (120 milliliters)
- 1 to 2 teaspoons borax or Tide detergent (5 to 10 milliliters)
- 2 plastic spoons, craft sticks, or other disposable stirrers
- 3 teaspoons water (15 milliliters)
- 4 teaspoons white or gel glue (20 milliliters)
- food coloring (optional)
- plastic or foam disposable plate
- 1 to 4 teaspoons corn starch (optional)
- plastic bag or container

4 When you are satisfied with the texture, spread and stretch the Frubbery material so it forms a skin. If you like, form it into a face. Poke a hole to make a "mouth" that's flexible enough to open and close.

5 You can also add corn starch to the mixture to make it drier. Put some in the cup with the glue, or sprinkle a little on the plate, roll the Frubbery blob in it, and knead.

6 Unlike real Frubber, this robot skin only holds its shape for a little while. If you leave it out to dry, it will lose its stretchiness in a few days. To save some Frubbery mixture to use again, store it in a plastic bag or container. It should last several weeks, and longer if refrigerated.

FUN FACTS

The Frubbery mixture can flow like a liquid, but it can also hold its shape like a solid. Some experimental soft robots designed to squeeze through tight openings can act like this too. This type of substance is called a **non-Newtonian fluid**. Ketchup, toothpaste, and shampoo are also non-Newtonian fluids!

ROBOT TEST PLATFORM

Robotics hobbyists and researchers can save time and money by buying or building a basic test platform. A robot test platform is designed to let you add different types of parts and change them easily. That way, you don't have to put together a robot from scratch every time you want to try out a new part. It can range from a simple base with wheels and perhaps a motor to a complete robot ready to be programmed. One common robot test platform design has two or more levels. The lower level has the power source and wheels, and the upper level is for sensors and electronics.

You can design your own robot test platform to use with some of the projects that come later in this book or for your own experiments. To get a ready-made rolling base, just remove the covering from a toy car or other vehicle. If you want it to move on its own, look for one with a pull-back spring mechanism or remote control. (Look back to the Introduction for tips on dismantling old electrical devices.) You can also design and build your own moving base. Wheels can be repurposed from old toys or devices, or make your own using bottle caps, coasters, and other recycled objects. Be sure to take pictures and keep notes on your materials and designs, so you have a record of what works and what needs improvement. Then build your own machine on top of the platform.

For the body, look at the list of possible robot-building materials at the end of the Introduction, or try some of these:

- **Metal**: breath mint tin, soda can, aluminum foil pie pan. Make sure no electrical connections or batteries touch the metal of the body.

- **Expanded plastic foam**: Styrofoam cups or plates, recycled food trays or packing material, cut up pool noodles, other floating toys.

- **Paper or cardboard**: corrugated cardboard from shipping boxes, cereal boxes or juice cartons, card stock, origami or scrapbook paper, papier-mâché.

- **Stiff plastic**: milk jugs, bottles, jars, reusable food containers, old plastic toys, clear plastic packaging from toys or other products, clear plastic hamster or tree ornament balls, candy tube-shaped containers, CDs or DVDs, computer mouse casing.

• **Rubber or soft stretchable plastic**: rubber ball (have an adult help cut open carefully with scissors or a knife), rubber bath toys, inflatable toys, balloons, soft baby teething or dog chew toys, bubble wrap.

• **Wood**: balsa wood (good for floating or flying robots), scrap lumber, craft sticks and shapes, bamboo placemats, paint stirrers, tree branches.

• **Soft fabric**: knitted sock or glove, stuffed doll or animal, felt cube or ball, ball of yarn, rip stop nylon from a kite or jacket.

And to hold everything together, you can try white or gel glue, puffy fabric or hot glue; rubber bands; plastic zip ties; wooden toothpicks, bamboo skewers, or dowels; twist ties, pipe cleaners, and other kinds of wire; clear, electrical, foam, duct, and other kinds of tape; hook and latch strips (like Velcro); paper clips, binder clips, or snack bag clips; nuts and bolts, screws, nails, thumb tacks, push pins, safety pins, and other hardware, office, or sewing supplies.

Meet RobotGrrl!

Erin Kennedy from Montreal, Canada, is also known as RobotGrrl. When she was 13, Erin began building robots on her own with LEGO Mindstorms. As a high school student in 2008, she was invited to study Artificial Intelligence at Stanford University in California. She paid for the trip by selling toy vibrobots she made from Styrofoam drinking cups. Her brightly colored Styrobots became famous on robotics web sites. Erin's more recent projects include RoboBrrd. Like many of Erin's creations, RoboBrrd's body is made from craft materials such as wooden craft sticks, felt, and feathers. She hopes to turn it into a programmable robot kit that younger students can make and decorate themselves.

Chapter 3 | ACTUATORS: MAKING ROBOTS MOVE

Just like living things, robots need energy to move and "think." Even the earliest automata that moved by themselves were powered by humans. People raised the weights, turned the cranks, and wound up the springs that made them move. But the power source for most modern robots is a ***battery***. The kind of batteries used in robots can range in size from tiny disks smaller than a dime to big, heavy car batteries the size of a cinder block.

A battery is a portable power plant that uses a chemical reaction to produce *electricity*.

How Does a Battery Produce Electricity?

In a battery, two metals made of different kinds of **atoms** are placed near each other in a container full of a special chemical. All atoms contain **electrons**, which have a negative charge. Negative charges **repel** other negative charges. They are attracted to positive charges. In the battery, one metal has a slight negative charge. The other metal has a slight positive charge. So the electrons from the negatively charged metal are attracted to the positively charged metal. The electrons travel through the chemical inside the container from one metal to the other. This movement creates a flowing negative charge, which we call electricity.

If a **circuit** is hooked up to the battery, the negative charge will flow out of the positive end, or **terminal**, of the battery, through the wires and components, and back into the battery through the negative terminal. The circuit has a **switch** that opens and closes like a drawbridge.

Words to Know

battery: a device that produces electricity using **chemicals**.

chemical: the pure form of a substance. Some chemicals can be combined or broken up to create new chemicals.

electricity: a form of energy released when electrons are in motion.

atoms: the extremely tiny building blocks that make up all chemicals.

electron: a part of an atom that has a negative charge. It can move from one atom to another.

repel: to push away.

circuit: a path that lets electricity flow when closed in a loop.

terminal: the point on a battery where electricity flows in or out.

switch: a device that controls the flow of electricity through a circuit.

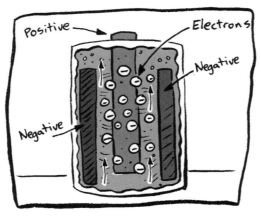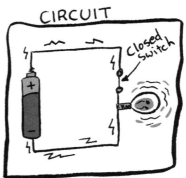

When the switch is open, no electricity can travel over the circuit. But when it is closed, the circuit is complete and the power starts humming!

A battery produces **direct current (DC)**. DC motors run on batteries. The electricity that flows through a wall outlet is **alternating current (AC)**. Some robots that don't move around can be plugged into AC outlets. Some kinds of batteries can also be plugged into AC rechargers when they have no more charge to flow, so they can be used again.

Words to Know

direct current (DC): electricity that flows in one direction.

alternating current (AC): electricity that flows back and forth at a steady rate.

solar cell: a device that converts the energy in light into electrical energy.

Solar Electricity

Another source of electricity for robots is the sun. A **solar cell** works somewhat like a battery, but it uses light rays from the sun to knock electrons off of atoms and set them in motion. NASA uses solar energy to keep the batteries in its Mars rovers charged.

A **BEAM** robot is a type of solar-powered machine that is popular with hobbyists. Robotics physicist Mark Tilden came up with the idea in 1989, by wondering what early robots would look like if they **evolved** like living things. The letters in BEAM stand for "biology" (because many BEAM robots are biomimetic), "electronics," "aesthetics" (which means "artistic"), and "mechanics."

Although BEAM robots use only simple circuits instead of computers, their unexpected movements make them act as if they are alive. Their secret is a capacitor, the electronic component that stores electricity like a battery.

The energy produced by the solar cell is stored in the capacitor until there is enough to make the robot's motor move. The time it takes to store enough energy depends on how much sunshine there is. When it's ready, the capacitor sends all its "juice" into the motor at once, and the robot jumps. To move again, the BEAM robot has to wait until its capacitor is recharged.

Words to Know

BEAM: a type of simple, solar-powered, lifelike robot controlled by a simple circuit.

evolve: a change in a species of living thing in response to the world around it.

**So look out! You never know when a
BEAM robot will come to life!**

Nuclear Power

For space robots traveling beyond the planet Mars, solar power just won't do. The sun is too far away to provide the amount of energy needed to keep their batteries charged. So NASA equips those robots with **nuclear** generators. These use the energy that releases when the center part of an atom, called its **nucleus**, splits apart.

Words to Know

nuclear: energy produced when the nucleus of an atom is split apart.

nucleus: the center of an atom.

radioactive: a substance made of atoms that gives off nuclear energy.

NASA launched the nuclear powered car-sized rover *Curiosity* in November 2011. Its **radioactive** fuel was designed to last a Martian year, which equals two Earth years. It will also provide more power than previous Mars rovers. The extra power will help this rover travel faster and climb over bigger obstacles.

Probably one of the strangest ways to power a robot is with the wind. Dutch artist Theo Jansen builds autonomous wind-powered walking machines called Strandbeests, or "beach animals." They consist of multiple pairs of legs made out of plastic tubes that step sideways across the sand. Propellers or sails collect the wind, which is stored in recycled lemonade bottles in the Strandbeest's belly. When the air pressure in the bottles is released, it powers the legs.

A narrow tube that Jansen calls a "feeler" drags along the ground and sucks in water when the Strandbeest gets too near the sea. This resets the machine's "brain" and makes it back up, toward land. Jansen's inventions take simple ideas and put them together in complex ways that make them shockingly lifelike.

Actuators: Power Systems

No matter where it gets its power, the part of a robot that makes it move is called an **actuator**. Robot builders use several different kinds of actuators. Simple robots can use DC motors. A DC motor has a shaft that spins around and around. To make it spin the other way, you have to reverse the electric current with a switch or reverse the batteries.

Words to Know

actuator: a piece of equipment that makes a robot move.

DIY: do-it-yourself.

Meet Robomaniac!

Robomaniac is the name used by Jérôme Demers on the web site Instructables.com. When he was only 16 years old, he invented a robot called a Beetlebot for a school science fair. The Beetlebot was a touch-sensitive BEAM robot that looked like a ladybug. It ran on DC motors from a recycled PlayStation video game console. Jérôme later shared the directions to build his Beetlebot on Instructables. His clever design led to a summer job working for a company called Solarbotics. They turned his Beetlebot into a **DIY** kit for beginning robot makers. Jérôme's inventions have since been featured in *The Absolute Beginner's Guide to Building Robots* by Gareth Branwyn and in *Make* magazine. Jérôme went on to study electrical engineering at the University of Sherbrooke in Canada.

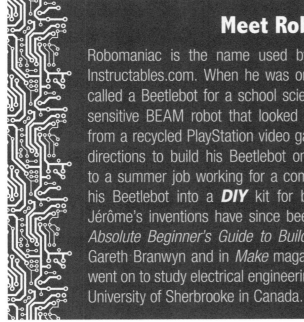

Motors are usually connected to machines by **gears**. Gears are wheels with interlocking teeth. They transfer the turning motion of the motor to the moving parts of the machine. Gears can also make the moving part go faster or slower than the motor, or give it more **force** or **torque**.

More advanced robots use a special kind of motor called a **servo**. Servos can be controlled electronically. The robot's controller tells the servo how far to turn, and in what direction. A servo can be used to make a robot's arm go up a certain amount and stop. Or it can make a robot turn its head back and forth. A six-legged robot will have a servo on each leg. The controller can be programmed to make the legs move separately or all together.

Some robots use other types of devices to make them move. **Hydraulic** systems use the force of a fluid such as water or oil, which is pushed through tubes by electric motors. They are very powerful, and are used by industrial robots that must lift heavy weights.

Words to Know

gears: wheels with interlocking teeth that transfer motion from one part of a machine to another.

force: a push or pull that changes the speed or direction of an object.

torque: the amount of force it takes to make something turn or spin.

servo: a motor that can be can be controlled electronically.

hydraulic: a system that pushes and pulls objects using tubes filled with fluid.

electromagnet: a temporary magnet created by running electricity through a magnet.

pneumatic: a system that pushes and pulls objects using tubes filled with air or other gases.

solenoid: an electromagnetic device that pushes a rod up and down.

How Motors Work

Motors work by using temporary *electromagnets*. When electricity flows through a wire, it becomes magnetic. But unlike permanent magnets, you can turn an electromagnet off by turning off the electricity. In a motor, the shaft—the part that spins—holds several electromagnetic coils of wire. Around it is a ring of permanent magnets. All magnets have a positive and a negative side, or pole. When you put one magnet near another magnet, their opposite poles pull toward each other, and their like poles push away from each other. Turn on a motor and the electromagnetic wire coils are pulled and pushed by the magnetic force of the permanent magnets around them. That pull and push makes the shaft spin, and the motor turns until you shut the power off.

COILS OF COPPER WIRE

MAGNETS

Pneumatic systems are similar, but they use air or other gasses instead of fluid. They are quieter than hydraulic systems, but not as strong. Pneumatics are often used to open and close robotic grippers. Both hydraulic and pneumatic systems use a *solenoid* to push a rod up and down.

The rod in turn pushes the oil or gas in the hydraulic or pneumatic system back and forth and moves the robot's parts.

Shape memory alloy wire can also move robot parts. It is made of a special combination of metals that can be heated by running an electric current through it. When heated, the wire shrinks. When the current is turned off, the wire cools and stretches to its original length.

The shrinking and stretching wire can be used like a puppet string to pull lightweight robotics parts up and down. Shape memory alloy is used in the cardboard cockroach robot, Dash. It has also been used to move earthworm-shaped robots from Taiwan and soft, wheel-shaped robots from Japan.

Getting Around: Drive Systems

Words to Know

caster: a wheel or ball-shaped roller that can swivel to point in any direction.

stability: how well something can stay in its proper position.

Some robots, especially those in factories, are built to stay in one place and have work brought to them. Other robots travel around to where they are needed. The most common way for robots to get around is on wheels. Many hobby robots have only two wheels with a support in front to keep them from tipping forward. The support can be a smaller wheel that rolls freely without a motor, a **caster**, or just a smooth knob that slides over the floor easily.

There are also two-wheeled balancing robots. They have sensors and controls that keep them shifting backward and forward so they don't tip over. Robots with three or four wheels can drive around like cars. For extra **stability**, some have more than four wheels. And rugged military robots often roll around on treads, just like tanks.

FUN FACTS

At Case Western Reserve University in Ohio, the Center for Biologically Inspired Robotics Research is working on robots with a cross between wheels and legs, called "whegs." Whegs look like spokes on a wheel. But instead of being connected by one round rim, each spoke has its own foot. The whegs help pull the robots over obstacles as they rotate.

Walking on two legs may be easy for humans, but not for robots. In humans, the brain automatically adjusts our bodies every time we move to keep us from falling over. To get a robot to balance while standing, walking, running, or going up stairs takes a lot of complicated programming.

One of the most well-known walking humanoid robots is ASIMO. The name stands for "Advanced Step in Innovative Mobility," which means it uses new ways to get around. The Honda car company developed ASIMO in 2000 and has been upgrading and improving it ever since. The latest version of ASIMO is able to catch itself when it loses its balance by quickly moving its feet.

That makes it possible for the robot to travel over uneven ground autonomously. ASIMO can also walk and run forward and backward. It can even hop!

Scientists are also working on creating robots that can climb. A six-legged robot named RiSE made by Boston Dynamics uses feet with micro-claws to climb up walls, trees, and fences. Its beaver-like tail helps it balance. At Stanford University, a team led by Professor Mark Cutkosky designed a robot called Stickybot that can climb up a window. It has feet like a gecko lizard that can stick to smooth surfaces but pull off easily.

47

BEAM-TYPE SOLAR WOBBLEBOT

This primitive BEAM-type robot has no "brain," but does react unpredictably to intense light by wobbling around on its one foot!

NOTE: This project uses a hot glue gun, so ask an adult for help.

SUPPLIES

- pencil with an eraser
- DC motor with wires attached
- solar panel (can be recycled from solar garden light)
- electrical tape
- scissors
- recycled CD or DVD
- hot glue gun
- tape
- recycled clear dome from drink cup

1 Break the eraser off the pencil. Use the point of the pencil to make a hole in the middle of the broken-off side. Push the eraser up onto the shaft of the motor. It will probably hold on well enough without glue.

2 If reusing a solar panel from a garden light, remove any batteries or capacitors and detach it from any other electronics inside. DO NOT cut the two wires coming from the solar panel itself!

3 Make sure the solar panel produces enough power to run the motor by temporarily connecting the wires with small pieces of electrical tape. Take it out in bright sunlight or hold the panel up to a very bright indoor light, such as a halogen light. If the motor doesn't turn, try another motor or a bigger solar panel. Once everything works, carefully take off the tape and separate the wires.

INVENTORY — TAPE, SOLAR PANEL, SCISSORS, PENCIL, DC MOTOR, CD, ELECTRICAL TAPE, GLUE GUN, CLEAR DOME

4 Hot glue the CD to the motor with the shaft sticking through the hole of the disk. Be careful not to get any glue into the motor or on the moving parts. Add some tape if needed for extra security.

HOT GLUE MOTOR TO CD

5 Place the clear dome top over the other end of the motor. Pull the motor wires through the hole at the top, where the straw would go. Glue the bottom of the dome onto the CD.

6 Attach the motor wires to the solar panel wires and tape them together securely. Then push the wires back in the dome and glue the solar panel on top.

7 Take the Solar WobbleBot outside in bright sunlight to test it. Put the bot with the disk-side down and the solar panel facing up (it will be just a little bit tilted), on a very smooth, flat surface, like a metal cookie sheet or the glossy cover of a book. Or ask an adult to help you use a very bright indoor light, like a halogen lamp or shop light. The motor shaft should spin and make the bot dance and skip around!

SIDE VIEW   WOBBLE   WOBBLE

Try This: Brainstorm a Better Robot

This WobbleBot works under ideal conditions, but it is just a prototype. What improvements could you add to make it more rugged or more reliable? Robot hobbyists and scientists are always sharing ideas for making better designs, so share yours with friends and see what you come up with together!

MODEL SOLENOID

Solenoids are electromagnetic coils wrapped around a tube with a metal plunger inside. When the electricity is turned on, a magnetic coil attracts the plunger and pulls it in. Sometimes permanent magnets are attached to the plunger. Then the electromagnet can also repel the plunger when it is turned on and push it out. Solenoids are used in many mechanisms such as car door locks. In robots, they can be used instead of a motor to push or pull an effector in a straight line. They can also be used to hit objects, like the keys in a robotic xylophone. This model shows how a solenoid uses electricity to move a plunger back and forth.

1 Cut a straw about 4 inches long (10 centimeters). Cut a piece of tape about 3 inches long (7½ centimeters). Fold one end over a couple times, sticky side out. Attach the sticky folded part to the straw, about ½ inch from one end so it hangs off like a flag (1 centimeter). Then wrap the rest of the tape around the straw, sticky side out.

2 Take the wire and let out about 6 inches (15 centimeters). Leave that wire hanging and start wrapping the rest of the wire around the straw over the tape. Start at one edge of the tape and go to the other edge, making a neat line of tight coils. Then, still coiling the wire in the same direction, make a second row on top of the first, going from the edge where you stopped back to the first edge.

Keep making layers of wire until you only have 6 inches left (15 centimeters). You should have at least 100 coils and two tails of wire left.

3 Take the battery and tape it across the other end of the straw to form a "T." If you are using magnet wire, take the sandpaper and rub off about ½ inch of the shiny coating from both ends (1 centimeter). If using regular wire, remove about ½ inch of insulation from both ends (1 centimeter). Tape one end of the wire to one end of the battery. Leave the other wire loose.

SUPPLIES

STRAW

WIRE

TAPE

SAND PAPER

BATTERY

NAIL

- plastic drinking straws
- electrical tape
- scissors
- 6 feet very thin insulated wire (2 meters)—size 32 magnet wire works best (available on spools at RadioShack)
- 1.5 volt battery (AAA works fine)
- sandpaper
- needle or thin nail
- super strong disk magnet (optional)
- flat head nail thin enough to fit in straw (optional)

4 Hold the straw upright about 1 inch from your work surface (2½ centimeters). Slip the needle, point up, into the straw and let it rest on the work surface. If you have a super strong disk magnet, you can use a nail instead of a needle. Let the magnet attach itself to the flat head of the nail. Insert the nail into the straw the same way.

5 Briefly touch the loose wire end to the other terminal of the battery. The needle should be pulled up into the straw. When you disconnect the battery, it drops down again. (If using a nail and magnet, you may have to flip the magnet over to make it work.)

PASSIVE DYNAMIC MINI-WALKER

A **passive dynamic** walker doesn't need a motor or actuator of any kind. Its only power source is the force of gravity! Also called a ramp walker, this system of walking works best on a slightly downward-tilted surface. Give it a little push and gravity will pull it downhill the rest of the way. This method of walking doesn't just save energy, it looks more natural too. Here is one way of making a small-scale passive dynamic walker. Experiment with different sizes and shapes, or use other materials that you have on hand. You can also try four legs instead of two, give your walker knees, or attach swinging arms to add energy to each step.

Words to Know

passive dynamic: a robot walker that is powered by gravity.

1 Cut out two legs from the cardboard, 2¾ inches long (7 centimeters) and 1½ inches wide (3 centimeters). From one end of each rectangle, measure 1 inch up (2½ centimeters) and make a ½ inch cut (1 centimeter). From there, trim up the cardboard so it forms an "L" shape, or a leg and a foot. With the pencil or nail, poke a hole at the top of each leg in the center. Fold the cardboard at the "ankle" so the foot sits flat.

2 Cut out two pieces craft foam, felt, or cork the same size as the foot. Glue it onto the bottom of each foot for padding and traction.

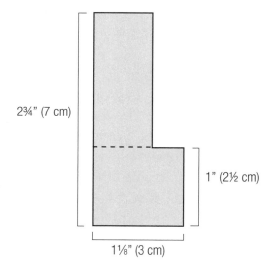

2¾" (7 cm)

1" (2½ cm)

1⅛" (3 cm)

3 Slip one of the beads onto the skewer a little past the middle. Try to use a bead that is a little tight on the skewer. If it's loose enough to slide around, just keep it in place with your finger for now.

BEADS

SUPPLIES

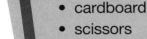

CRAFT STICKS

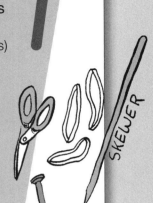

SCISSORS

SKEWER

- cardboard
- scissors
- sharp pencil or large nail about as wide around as the skewer
- 1 small sheet craft foam, felt, or thin cork (peel-and-stick is best)
- glue stick
- bamboo skewer about 10 inches long (25 centimeters)

- wooden or plastic beads
- mini craft sticks about 2½ inches (6½ centimeters) long, or regular craft sticks or coffee stirrers cut to size
- clear tape or 2 rubberbands (optional)
- large sheet foam core (optional)
- masking tape (optional)

4 Slide one of the legs onto the skewer through the hole so that the foot faces the end of the skewer with the bead. The leg and the bead should be almost touching.

5 Slide one big bead or several small beads onto the skewer so they are just touching the inside of the first leg. The bead(s) should cover about ½ inch of the skewer (1 centimeters).

6 Slide on the second leg so that the front of the foot is pointing in the same direction as the first foot. Slip another bead onto the skewer to hold the legs in place, making sure there is just enough space for the legs to swing back and forth easily. If the outside beads are not staying in place, wrap a rubber band or a little piece of tape around the skewer to keep them from sliding around.

7 Stick a bead on each end of the skewer. It should be tight enough to stay on. If not, attach with tape. You can glue the beads on, but first make sure the legs are in the center of the skewer and your mini-walker is balanced. Avoid getting any glue on the legs!

8 Stand the walker on its feet. Glue a mini-craft stick onto each foot, right next to the leg.

9 Make a test ramp with a long flat surface that you can tilt slightly, like a big book or a sheet of stiff cardboard. Foam core makes a nice walking surface. For added traction put some strips of masking tape down the length of your ramp. To test the walker, set it at the top of the ramp and gently tap one end of the skewer. The walker should tip from side to side as it makes its way downhill.

EFFECTORS: HOW ROBOTS DO THINGS

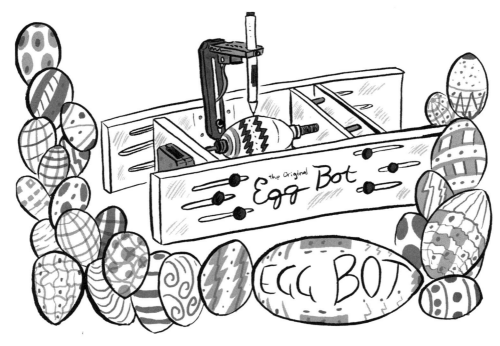

Anything a robot uses to affect the outside world is called an effector. An effector might be an arm, gripper, tool, weapon, light, or speaker.

On an industrial robot arm, an effector can be a paint gun or a welder. One of the effectors on NASA's Mars rovers was a tool to grind up rock samples from the planet's surface. Robots that draw, like our Art-Making Vibrobot, use pens for effectors. So does the Eggbot, a programmable robot that draws detailed designs on eggshells.

FUN FACTS

One suggested hack for the Eggbot drawing machine lets you control it by turning the dials on an Etch A Sketch!

For a household robot, an effector can be a vacuum, mower blade, or a mop. In a smart home, effectors can be overhead lights, stereo systems, and other built-in appliances with robotic controls.

Other kinds of robot effectors work by copying a person's movements. They can follow the movements exactly, or they can make them bigger or smaller. The da Vinci Surgical System senses the movements of a doctor's hands on the machine's controls. Then it transmits them to its effectors, which are miniature medical instruments on its arms. These tiny tools actually do the operation, with the doctor and the da Vinci robot brain working together. Right now a surgeon controls the da Vinci by moving a handle around. But in experiments at Johns Hopkins University in Baltimore, computer scientist Gregory Hager's team has used a Kinect motion detector to let a doctor control the surgical instruments just by making gestures in the air.

The Kinect can sense how a person's hands are moving, just as it does when it is used to play video games on the Xbox.

Want a Ride on a Mech?

A mech is like a super-sized powered exoskeleton, big enough for a person to ride inside. Sakakibara Kikai, a Japanese company that builds farm machinery, also makes mechs for fun. The Kid's Walker is a child-sized mech. It has two enormous arms with large metal clamps as effectors. Its two thick legs have wheels that act like roller skates to move it along smoothly. To drive the Kid's Walker, the human user climbs into a seat in the robot's chest, high off the ground. Then the user steers it with two joysticks built into the seat's armrests. Sakakibara Kikai also makes fighting robots it calls MechBoxers. They look a little like life-sized Rock'em Sock'em Robot toys. But instead of controlling the punching with levers on the outside of a small plastic boxing ring, the user sits inside its mechanical MechBoxer. There are foot pedals to control the movement and buttons on a handle to place punches. Meanwhile, the human drivers are protected by the metal skeleton of the machines!

Hello!

A powered exoskeleton that magnifies the user's motions is another kind of effector. Some, like the ReWalk, help disabled people move more naturally. Others work like a robotic suit to give a person with ordinary abilities extra strength and speed.

In 2010, the Raytheon Company of Massachusetts unveiled a new version of its XOS Exoskeleton. A person wearing the XOS can lift loads as heavy as a large man for long periods of time without getting tired. According to Raytheon, one person in an exoskeleton suit can do the work of two or three people.

Degrees of Freedom

Effectors and other parts of the robot that can move around have different **degrees of freedom**. Each direction in which a robotic part can move is one degree of freedom. An arm that can only move up and down has one degree of freedom. If it can also move side to side, it has two degrees of freedom. And if it can also rotate around in either direction, it has three. Each degree of freedom usually needs a **joint** and an actuator to move it. The joint allows the robot part to move in one or more ways.

Words to Know

degrees of freedom: the number of directions in which a robotic effector or other part can move.

joint: a place on a robot arm or other part where it can bend or turn.

A robot arm with three degrees of freedom can usually reach anything within its area.

Even more degrees of freedom can sometimes make it more useful. The typical robotic arm, like the Canadarm on the International Space Station, has six degrees of freedom. Like a human arm, it has shoulder, elbow, and wrist joints. The shoulder can move up and down as well as side-to-side, so it has two degrees of freedom. The elbow can move up and down, so it has one degree of freedom. The wrist has can move up and down, side-to-side, and turn, so it has three degrees of freedom. This makes a total of six degrees of freedom along the entire arm.

It might seem like adding more degrees of freedom would be a good thing. But each extra degree of freedom makes the robot more complicated to build. All the different movements have to be powered and controlled so they all work together.

That's why robot designers usually try to include the fewest degrees of freedom needed for the robot to do its job.

However, researchers are working on new and more advanced machines with many more degrees of freedom. A German company called Festo makes a Bionic Handling Assistant that can curl and bend like an elephant's trunk. The arm has 13 pneumatic actuators and 11 degrees of freedom. But the whole thing is made out of rings of flexible plastic, so there are no joints. At the end of the "trunk" is a three-fingered FinGripper. The finger design is based on the fin of a fish. It can handle objects that regular robotic arms might bruise or break, such as oranges, eggs, and bottles.

The Universal Jamming Gripper is an experimental effector that uses a totally different kind of design. It works on the principle of "jamming." When rough grains of material such as sand are loose, they flow like a liquid. But when they're packed tightly together, they act like one solid mass.

The Universal Jamming Gripper is made from a latex party balloon filled with ground-up coffee beans. The coffee-filled balloon is attached to a vacuum. To pick up an object, the balloon is pressed down on it. Then the vacuum sucks the air out of the balloon, causing the coffee grounds to pack together tightly around the object and hold it. In tests, the Universal Jamming Gripper was strong enough to lift two large jugs of water, and flexible enough to pick up a penny lying flat on the table.

ROBOTIC HAND

It's a hard job to design a robotic hand that can pick up an object without damaging it. Robotic hands usually have dozens of mechanical joints. Each joint has a servo motor that must be programmed to handle specific objects. In 2010, mechanical engineering professor Aaron Dollar and the Grab Lab at Yale University in Connecticut created a new kind of hand. It was made of soft plastic and rubber and worked like a human hand. A single motor pulled different wires to make the fingers bend. The wires acted like tendons, the strings in a human hand that help muscles move. This cardboard version also uses pull-strings to make the fingers open and close realistically.

SUPPLIES

- 1 sheet of card stock (stiff postcard-type paper) or other thin, stiff cardboard
- scissors
- marker
- clear tape
- 3–4 drinking straws
- 5 pieces of string, each about 10 inches long (25 centimeters)
- crochet hook (optional)

1 For the palm of your robot hand, cut out a 4-inch square of cardboard (10 centimeter square).

2 For the fingers, cut out four rectangles, each ¾ inch wide (2 centimeters) and 3 inches long (7½ centimeters). Cut out a rectangle 1 inch wide (2½ centimeters) and 2 inches long (5 centimeters) for the thumb. Draw horizontal lines to divide each finger and the thumb into 1-inch sections (2½ centimeters). These are the joints.

3 Lay out your robot hand by lining up the fingers along the top of the palm and the thumb on the side.

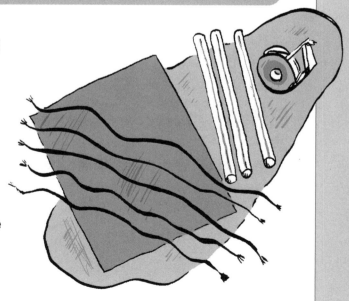

4 Cut the fingers and thumb into sections along the joint lines. Reassemble, leaving a little space between each section.

5 Use tape to connect the finger sections to each other and to the palm, making sure to keep a space between each section. Tape the front and back for extra strength.

6 Cut the straws into 19 pieces about ½ inch long (1½ centimeters).

7 On the inside of the hand, tape one piece of straw onto each finger section and onto the palm below each finger. Trim the tape if needed, so it doesn't hang over the edge of the straw.

8 Thread one string through the straws for each finger. (A crochet hook will help you pull the string through the straws.) Tape the end of the string over the tip of the finger, leaving the lower end hanging loose.

9 Pull the strings to curl the fingers inward. With a little practice you'll be able to make your robot hand point or pick up objects with amazingly lifelike gestures.

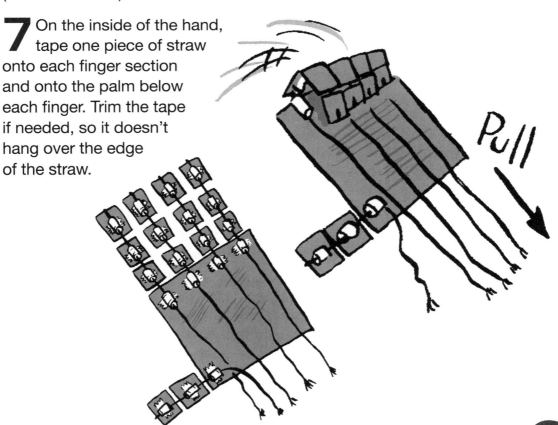

Pull

ROBOTIC ARM

This robotic arm has only two degrees of freedom but it can still bend down and pick up objects. It uses hydraulic power to move each joint. This system uses plastic syringes, cardboard, and duct tape. You can also adapt this design to use a building set like LEGO or K'nex, or other kinds of materials like wooden paint stirrers and craft sticks. Or increase the degrees of freedom by adding a swivel base that turns back and forth, another arm section that bends up and down, or a gripper that opens and closes.

SUPPLIES

- stiff cardboard, enough to build an arm and a base
- scissors
- 2 cardboard paper towel tubes
- duct tape
- sharpened pencil stub
- ¼-inch-wide clear rubber tubing (6.3 millimeters) **that fits over the tip of the syringes, about 6 feet long** (2 meters)
- clear tape, preferably strong packing tape
- 4 oral syringes, 10 milliliter size, with rubber ring on plunger if possible (often given out free at drug stores)
- water
- 2 colors liquid food coloring
- foam tape (optional)

1 Make a large square base for your robotic arm out of a flat piece of cardboard. Also cut two long strips of cardboard for the side pieces of the arm. These should be about as wide and long as the paper towel tubes. Cover all the flat pieces, as well as the cardboard tubes, with duct tape.

2 Take one of the paper towel tubes to make a tower to hold the arm. About 2 inches from one end (5 centimeters), take the pencil and poke it straight through the tube so it sticks out both sides. This is the bottom of the tower. Pull the pencil out. Poke another hole about 1 inch above one of the first holes (2½ centimeters),

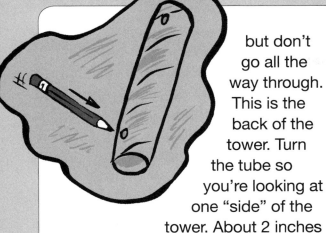

but don't go all the way through. This is the back of the tower. Turn the tube so you're looking at one "side" of the tower. About 2 inches from the top (5 centimeters), poke the pencil straight through from side to side, then remove it.

3 Cut a piece of rubber tubing about 2 feet long (60 centimeters). Thread it straight through the bottom set of holes so some tubing is sticking out both ends. Cut a second piece 3 feet long (1 meter). Thread it into the single hole near the bottom and out through the top. Tape the bottom of the tower to the base near one end with the front of the tower facing toward the nearest edge.

4 Hold the end of one of the side pieces over one of the holes in the top of the tower. Take the pencil and poke a hole through the side piece and through both holes in the tower. Leave it there as a rod to hold the arm. Line the other side piece up with the first and push it onto the pencil point. Break the point off the pencil, or cover it with tape.

5 Label the syringes #1, #2, #3, and #4. To make the arm, take the other paper towel tube and lay it down. Lay syringe #1 along the tube so the end of the plunger hangs off the end of the tube. Use clear packing tape to secure the syringe to the tube. Cover the ends of the clear tape with duct tape for a better hold, but keep the middle clear so you can watch the pump in action.

TAPE

TAPE SYRINGE TO THE END OF THE ARM

continues on next page . . .

7 To move the arm up and down, connect syringe #3 to the shorter piece of tubing coming out the bottom of the tower in front. Pull its plunger out almost all the way. Position the arm out straight with the plunger holding it up. Use a piece of tape to hold the pump to the tower in this position. If you use clear tape, add duct tape over the edges to keep them in place. Connect the other end of the tubing coming out the back to syringe #4 to make another control pump.

6 Position the tube between the side pieces of the arm with the plunger facing away from the tower. Move it so that the end of the plunger almost touches the table when the arm is down, but the tube doesn't hit the tower. Duct tape the tube in place between the arms. Attach the tubing coming out of the top of the tower to the tip of the syringe. Connect the other end of the same tubing to syringe #2 to make a control pump.

8 Test the system using pneumatic power. Push in the plunger on one control pump. Make sure the plunger at the other end of the tubing slides out. If there's no rubber ring and air is leaking in, take out the plungers and try wrapping a very small rubber band or the ring from the end of a rubber balloon near the end. Replace the plungers.

9 To test for hydraulic power, fill the tubes with water. Pull the plunger out of syringe #2. Make sure the plunger at the other end is pressed in as far as it can go. Hold the open syringe upright and fill it with water. Add a few drops of food coloring. Then replace the plunger and push it in all the way. Now pick up the arm by the base and turn it sideways, so syringe #1 is pointing up. Remove its plunger, and fill the remaining space with water. Replace the plunger. Turn the arm and put it back on its base, so it is right side up again. Slowly push the water back and forth a few times. If necessary, repeat these steps to let air bubbles escape or add more water. Be careful not to overfill the system or it will make the plunger pop out of the pump! When you have one system working, do the same with the other, using a different color for the water.

10 When everything's working, tape down the control pumps to the base so their plungers hang off the end. Then press in syringe #4 to raise the arm until it is sticking straight out. Place a small piece of foam tape on the underside of the arm where the plunger on syringe #3 touches the arm to keep it from sliding too far out of place. (You can also connect the plunger to the arm with a loose piece of duct tape.)

11 Finally, test your robotic arm. Find a lightweight object with a large opening, loop, or hook. See if you can make the arm bend down and pick it up. It may take a little practice to push the right pump at the right time!

SOFT ROBOTIC GRIPPER

Making your own version of the Universal Jamming Gripper is easy. If you don't have a vacuum pump handy, you can just use your lungs. But the smell of coffee grounds is pretty strong, so you may prefer to try this version, which uses sugar.

1 Make a funnel by cutting the soda bottle a little below the "shoulder." Take the top half, turn it upside down, and set it in the bottom half.

2 Blow up the balloon to stretch it, and then let the air out. Fit the opening of the balloon onto the neck of the soda bottle funnel. Place the funnel back in the bottom of the soda bottle, with the balloon hanging down in the bottle.

3 Pour the sugar through the funnel into the opening of the balloon. Squeeze in as much as you can.

SUPPLIES

- clean, empty soda bottle
- scissors
- latex balloon
- about 1/2 cup granular table sugar (100 grams)
- sturdy plastic straw
- small piece of thin cloth (an old T-shirt works well), about 2 inches square (5 square centimeters)
- electrical tape

5 To test your robotic gripper, press and shape the balloon over an object you want to pick up, such as a bottle cap. Then put the top end of the straw in your mouth and suck out as much air as you can. Keep sucking on the straw as you try to lift the object. Then breathe out and let the object drop. See how many different shapes you can pick up with your gripper!

4 Cover the bottom end of the straw with the cloth. Secure the cloth to the straw with tape. Make sure it's on tightly. Insert the cloth end of the straw into the balloon through the funnel so the rubber covers all the cloth. Carefully remove the balloon from the funnel and pinch the top around the straw. Lift the funnel up and off the straw. Secure the balloon to the straw by winding more tape around it.

Chapter 5

SENSORS: HOW ROBOTS KNOW WHAT'S GOING ON

Robots, like living things, use their senses to figure out what is happening around them. For humans, those senses include seeing, hearing, touching, smelling, and tasting.

To see, your eyes take in information in the form of light waves and convert it into electrical signals that your brain can understand. To hear, your ears detect sound waves, and your brain figures out if what you're listening to is words, music, or just noise. When you use your nose, you're sampling particles of something floating around in the air. Tasting with your tongue gives you useful clues about what chemicals something contains. Touching with your skin tells you what an object's surface is like and whether it's hot or cold. You can also feel through your bones and muscles. You get an idea of how heavy something is when you lift it, or if you feel the ground shake when an object falls or rumbles past you.

A robot's sensors are mechanical or electronic, but they work very much like ours.

They take in information and convert it into an electrical signal that the robot's brain can understand. The information the sensor collects is called **input**. The robot's "brain" takes the input and decides what to do, based on its design or program. Then the robot uses its effectors to respond. That response is called the robot's **output**.

FUN FACTS

Tigers, seals, and rats use their whiskers to feel things they brush up against. Robots can use artificial whiskers as touch sensors, too. In dark or dusty conditions or underwater, whiskers work better than light sensors or cameras. They're also cheaper to replace if they break. NASA researchers have experimented with whiskers on their Mars rovers.

Words to Know

input: a signal or information that is put into a machine or electrical system.

output: the movement or other response of a robot to the input it receives from its sensors.

The simplest kind of robotic sensor is a mechanical switch, such as a push button or a **lever** that you slide. A switch can be used as a touch sensor by mounting it on the outside of the robot. It can be designed or programmed to turn the robot off or make it change direction if the robot bumps into something that presses the switch.

Words to Know

lever: a bar or handle used to run or adjust something.

photoresistor: a light sensor that works by changing the resistance in an electrical current depending on the amount of light.

ultraviolet (UV): a type of light with a shorter wavelength than visible light, also called black light.

Another simple sensor is a tilt switch. It activates when a robot leans over. One type of tilt switch is a tube with a small metal ball inside. The ball rolls back and forth in the tube as it is tipped one way or the other. Across one end of the tube are two wires. The wires are the ends of an electrical circuit. Because the wires are not touching, the circuit is open and no electricity can get through. But if a robot leans over far enough, it turns the tube so that the wires are at the bottom.

Then the metal ball rolls down, touches both wires, closes the circuit, and sends an electrical signal to the robot.

Lights, Camera, Action!

Robots can also use different kinds of light sensors, such as a **photoresistor**, that act like an electronic eye. A resistor is an electronic device that controls how much electricity flows through it. A photoresistor uses light to control the electricity flow.

The photoresistor consists of a small disk with a squiggly line painted on it that is connected to an electrical circuit. The line is made of a chemical that is sensitive to light. When light hits the chemical the resistance goes down and more electricity flows through the circuit. The lower the

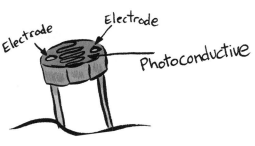

resistance, the better it conducts electricity. So a photoresistor lets the robot know when it's in the shade or in bright light.

Many animals have the ability to sense things humans can't. Robots have sensors that can do that, too. **Ultraviolet (UV)** light is normally invisible to human eyes, but some insects and birds can see it. Some flowers attract bees with colors and patterns only visible in UV light. Have you ever seen something glow under a "black light" bulb? That glow comes from the bulb's UV radiation.

FUN FACTS

Light sensors can also be used like a primitive type of camera. Put a bunch of them together, and a robot can use the input to decide if the patterns of dark and light make up a symbol it can "read."

71

Build Your Own
ROLLING BALL TILT SENSOR

This tilt sensor can be used to trigger effectors that work with a simple on/off switch. You can test it with a motor or LED bulb. Or, if you have a small speaker from a noisemaking toy, you can turn it into a buzzer just by running electricity through the wires. One fun device to try is the electrical sound mechanism from a greeting card. When you open the card, it plays music or a message you record. Attach it to your tilt sensor and it will start to play when the sensor is tipped over!

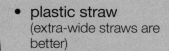

SUPPLIES

- plastic straw (extra-wide straws are better)
- scissors
- 1 to 3 metal ball bearings small enough to fit inside the straw (look for them at hardware stores or a bike shop)
- 2 small or medium safety pins

- tape (clear or electrical)
- 1 foot insulated electrical wire (30 centimeters)
- wire stripper (optional)
- greeting card with sound or other electrical effector
- battery (if not already attached to above)

1 Cut a straight piece of straw about 3 inches long (7 centimeters). Cover one end with a small piece of tape, sticky side up, or paper. Secure with a larger piece of tape. Place one or more balls inside the straw.

STEP TWO

2 Stick two safety pins through the other end of the straw about ½ inch from the end (1 centimeter). They should look like bars across a window. Make sure to leave some space between the safety pins inside the straw. Also check that the pins cannot touch each other on the outside of the straw.

3 Roll the ball down toward the safety pins. Make sure the ball can touch both safety pins at the same time. If not, move the pins until it does.

4 Cut two pieces of wire, each about 6 inches long (15 centimeters). Use the wire stripper or scissors to strip about ½ inch of insulation off both ends of each wire so that the metal is exposed (1 centimeter). Attach one end of a wire to the clasp end of one safety pin. Secure with tape. Do the same with the other wire and pin.

5 To use a greeting card sound device, open the card and carefully unfold the glued flap that hides the sound mechanism. Detach the plastic sliding pull arm from the metal on/off switch. The switch has a metal tab that touches a metal plate. Bend the tab up to turn it off. You can tape the tilt switch (the straw) right to the card, or carefully cut the entire sound mechanism out of the card to use it separately. Use tape to connect one wire from the tilt switch to the metal tab. Attach the other wire to the metal plate.

6 If you want to use a different kind of electrical effector (light, buzzer, or motor) that doesn't have its own battery, cut two pieces of wire, strip the insulation off the ends, and attach one piece to each terminal of the battery. Then attach one of the loose ends to one of the safety pins. Attach the other to one of the metal leads or wires coming off the effector. Connect the other metal lead to the other safety pin with another piece of wire.

7 To test the tilt switch, tip it so the ball is touching both safety pins. The effector should turn on. If not, check all the connections. When everything works, secure all connections with tape.

MISTER ROBOTO!

UV rays from the sun make our skin tan or burn. In some homes, UV light sensors are used in heating furnaces. They act like fire alarms by detecting the UV light from a flame. Some home heating units use UV light sensors like fire alarms. They can tell if the flame in the unit's pilot light is working by measuring its UV radiation. These kinds of UV sensors are used by robots in the Fire Fighting Home Robot competition for sixth grade through high school students at Trinity College in Connecticut.

FUN FACTS

Some people can sense ultraviolet light. The human eye has a lens that normally protects the eye from sun damage by absorbing UV rays. People who are missing that lens can see what bees see!

I'm On My Way

With **sonar**, robots can use sound waves to tell how far away something is. Bats and whales use sonar to locate objects in the dark or underwater. The animals make sounds and then listen for an **echo**, which is the same sound bouncing off an object and coming back to the place it was made. The longer it takes for the echo to reach them, the farther away the object.

A sonar sensor on a machine bounces sound waves off of objects in the same way. Robotic cars like the Lexus LS 460 L use sonar to steer around objects. It helps the car park itself without hitting anything nearby.

Words to Know

sonar: a way to detect objects by bouncing sound waves off them and measuring how long it takes to detect an echo.

echo: sound waves that bounce off a distant object and reflect back to the place they started.

The same echo technique is used in **radar**, which bounces radio waves or microwaves off an object, and **lidar**, which uses laser or other light waves.

Robots can also use **infrared (IR)** light waves to measure distance. Like UV light, IR rays are invisible to the human eye. But we can feel IR light—as heat! Infrared lamps are sometimes used by restaurants to keep food warm. Animals that can detect IR radiation "see" different temperatures the same way we see different colors. For instance, rattlesnakes have IR "pits" near their nose that help them hunt after dark. The pits can detect the IR light radiating off of warm-blooded animals.

Robots can use IR sensors like snakes do, to detect heat. But they can also use an IR **emitter** and an IR sensor together just like sonar. The emitter sends out one or more beams of IR light, and the sensor measures how long it takes for the light rays to bounce back off the object in front of them. The Xbox Kinect video game console uses IR light this way to tell where your body, arms, and legs are as you move around.

Words to Know

radar: a device that detects objects by bouncing microwaves or radio waves off them and measuring how long it takes for the waves to return.

lidar: a device that measures distance by shining light at an object and measuring the time it takes for the light to reflect back.

infrared (IR): a type of light with a longer wavelength than visible light, which can also be felt as heat.

emitter: a device that emits, or sends out, a light or sound wave or other signal.

75

Robots can also navigate around using the same kind of devices we use, but theirs are usually built in. A robotic compass can tell a robot the direction it's heading, just like a compass hikers use. Robots also use **GPS** to determine where they are on Earth.

Some robots come equipped with cameras and microphones that can transmit signals to human operators over short or long distances. After an earthquake and flooding damaged a nuclear power plant in Japan in 2011, the level of radiation was unsafe for humans. So a pair of iRobot PackBots was sent in. PackBots are military bomb-detecting robots that are built to withstand harsh conditions. The robots sent back video and other information about the damage.

Mobile **telepresence** robots don't usually go into hazardous areas, but they work the same way. In 2011, a Texas high school student named Lyndon who became too sick to go to school began using a telepresence robot to attend classes.

The robot, built by VGo Communications, has a microphone and camera so Lyndon can see and hear what is going on at school. It also has a speaker and video screen that lets teachers and classmates see and hear Lyndon.

A Self-Driving Car Uses Its Senses

In 2010, the Internet search company Google announced that it had been testing a self-driving car on roads in California. The car was developed by computer scientist Sebastian Thrun of Stanford University. Thrun led the team that built Stanley, the first car to finish the DARPA Grand Challenge for driverless vehicles in 2005. Thrun hopes that robotic cars will someday help prevent accidents and traffic jams. The Google car uses video cameras, sonar, GPS, and other sensors to detect traffic, obstacles, and people around it. It sends the input to Google's computers to analyze. The Google car has already driven itself hundreds of thousands of miles through crowded cities and on twisting mountain roads. Look out for it if you're on Highway 101 in Silicon Valley!

Lidar

Video Camera

R

Lyndon drove the robot from room to room at his high school by remote control from his home computer. The robot let Lyndon feel like he was still in school. It helped his classmates feel like he was there too.

To measure acceleration, which is a change in speed or direction of a moving object, a robot can use an **accelerometer**. This device works by detecting tiny movements in a weight, magnet, or air bubble.

77

Words to Know

smartphone: a mobile phone that can also be used like a simple computer to play games, send email, watch movies, etc.

tablet: a small, flat portable computer with a touchscreen instead of a keyboard for entering information.

Accelerometers are built into many kinds of devices today. When you turn a **smartphone**, iPad, or **tablet** sideways, the accelerometer turns the image on the display screen around to match. The Nintendo Wii video game uses an accelerometer in its controller to detect how you move it.

An accelerometer activates the airbag in a car if it stops suddenly in a crash. On a robot, an accelerometer can measure its speed and the distance it has gone. It can also tell when the robot starts and stops moving, when it has crashed into something, and whether it is tilted or straight.

Try This: Turn a Tilt Sensor into an Accelerometer

You can make a simple accelerometer using the same design as the tilt sensor project on page 72. Instead of sealing off one end, put safety pins at both ends. Then mount it on some kind of base (such as a piece of cardboard) or directly to a rolling toy or robot. Hook up each end of the accelerometer tube to an electrical effector, such as a speaker or LED. You'll need two this time—one for the front, one for the back. If you need to add a battery, both effectors can be wired to the same one.

Now make the accelerometer move quickly backward or forward. When it moves forward, the ball should roll backward and turn on the effector at the back end. You may need to try using different lengths of straw and more than one ball to get a better effect.

The accelerometer works because of the First Law of Motion described by Sir Isaac Newton in 1687. It says an object at rest tends to stay at rest. The accelerometer starts to move, but the ball tries to stay in the same spot. So the ball is not really rolling backward—the straw is moving forward underneath it!

USE A DIGITAL CAMERA AS AN INFRARED DETECTOR

When you point a remote at a television and press a button, you're sending an infrared light signal to an IR detector built into the TV set. But that light is invisible to humans—unless you've got a digital camera!

SUPPLIES

- TV remote
- digital camera or cell phone with camera
- a friend
- Kinect for Xbox motion-sensing device (optional)

1 To see the IR emitter on your TV remote light up, hold it in front of the lens of a digital camera or cell phone camera. Have a friend hold the remote for you. Get as close as you can and still be in focus.

REMOTE

DIGITAL CAMERA

A FRIEND

2 Watch the display screen on your camera as your friend presses any of the buttons on the TV remote. You should be able to see it flash on and off. It will look slightly purple.

3 The Kinect motion sensor for the Xbox game console also uses IR light. If you have a Kinect, you can use this same method to see the IR light beams. Darken the room, turn on the machine, and take a look around through your camera. You should be able to see hundreds of sparkling dots of light covering everything around you!

CLICK

Build Your Own

PRESSURE SENSOR

A pressure sensor is a type of touch sensor. It works as a resistor. The harder it is pressed, the more electricity can flow through. A robotic hand with pressure sensors on its surface or skin can tell how tightly or gently it is holding an object. On the bottom of a robot's foot, a pressure sensor signals when the foot has touched the ground.

In this activity, the pressure sensor turns an LED lightbulb on and off when you press on it. Push down lightly and the light will be dim and flicker. Push down hard and the light will glow steady and bright.

1 Test the LED with the battery to make sure it works. Slip the battery between the metal legs, or leads, of the LED bulb. Make sure the positive side of the battery faces the longer lead.

2 Take a piece of aluminum foil bigger than the two cards together and place the shiny side down on your work surface. Use the glue stick to completely cover one side of each card with glue. Then take each card and stick it firmly to the aluminum foil.

3 Cut around the cards on the foil, trimming a little bit off the edges of the card. When you're done, the foil should be the exact same size as the cards.

SUPPLIES

- 1 LED lightbulb with two metal legs
- 1, 3-volt disk battery (like a watch battery)
- aluminum foil
- 2 index cards or other pieces of thin cardboard
- glue stick
- scissors
- clear or electrical tape
- permanent marker
- yarn or thick string
- gel glue
- toothpick
- tissue

INVENTORY

SCISSORS

GLUE

LED BULB

3-VOLT BATTERY

INDEX CARDS

YARN

Aluminum Foil

GEL GLUE

PEN

TAPE

4 Take one of the cards and put it foil side up in front of you. Take the LED and tape the longer lead to the foil side of the card so the bulb is hanging off the edge of the card. The other lead should be up in the air. Take the battery and place it in the middle of the card. With the marker, trace around it on the foil. Remove the battery. Then draw a line all the way around the card just inside the edge. When you get to the LED go around it, leaving some room. Draw a spiral circle from the middle to the line around the outside edge.

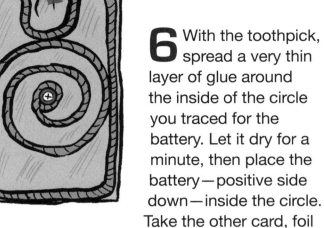

5 Cut a piece of yarn about 1 foot long (30 centimeters). Squeeze a line of gel glue on all the marker lines. Then take one end of the yarn and start to lay it along the line of glue. Use the toothpick to push the yarn down into the glue. Cut the yarn where needed. Clean up any glue outside the lines with a tissue. Let it dry.

6 With the toothpick, spread a very thin layer of glue around the inside of the circle you traced for the battery. Let it dry for a minute, then place the battery—positive side down—inside the circle. Take the other card, foil side down, and place it over the first card so the edges match. Tape the other leg of the LED to the top card. The LED should be off when you are not touching it. If it lights up, push the battery down so it is not touching the top card.

7 Now test the pressure sensor by pressing on the card. The LED should start to glow. Try different spots to see which work best. When everything's working, tape the edges of the cards together with small pieces of tape. Don't squeeze the cards while you're taping.

81

HACK A LINE-FOLLOWING ROBOT CAR

Roboticists can be very creative in the way they get one kind of sensor to do more than one kind of task. On a **line-following** robot, a photoresistor lets a robot "see" a dark line on a light-colored floor. On a **photovore** robot, the same sensor tells it to move toward the area with the brightest light.

You can try using a photoresistor in different ways by hacking an inexpensive robotic toy called the Doodle Track Car. The Doodle Track Car works just like a line-following robot. On its underside are two light sensors, one for each side. Each sensor controls a motor that turns the rear wheel on its side of the car. If the sensor detects light, it lets the motor run. If there is no light, it makes the motor stop. So if the line bends to the right, it will pass under the right sensor and make the right rear wheel stop. Since the left rear wheel is still pushing the car, the whole thing pivots to the right. That keeps the car centered over the line.

The Doodle Track Car is very cool as is. But if you're daring and don't mind dismantling your toy, you can turn it into a photovore robot.

Words to Know

line-following: a robot that uses sensors to detect and follow a line on the ground.

photovore: a robot that chases light.

1 Turn the car over. Open the battery compartment with the Phillips screwdriver and insert the batteries. Find the two black plastic bumps with slits. These are the car's light sensors. Now turn the power switch to "on" and shine the flashlight on the sensors. Try covering one sensor at a time with your finger. Notice how covering one sensor makes the wheel on that side stop turning. Turn the switch to "off."

SUPPLIES

- 1 Doodle Track Car (at toy stores or from Amazon or doodletrackcar.com)
- narrow Phillips head screwdriver
- flashlight
- 2 AAA batteries
- small flat head screwdriver
- small piece of cardboard
- tape
- 3-volt disk battery (optional)

2 Remove the car's cover by taking out the four screws on the car's underside. You can also unscrew and remove the front wheels—they aren't needed. If you want to make the Doodle Track Car into a line-following robot, you can simply replace the original cover with a robot-shaped body. (See the Junkbot directions in Chapter 2 for suggestions.) Make sure your new cover doesn't get in the way of the wires, the wheels, or the light sensors. Try it out on a black line you print or draw.

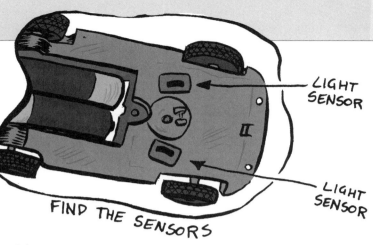

FIND THE SENSORS

LIGHT SENSOR

LIGHT SENSOR

3 To hack the car into a photovore robot, the next step is to switch the motors around. That way, when the sensor on one side detects light, the wheel on the opposite side will keep turning so the car pivots toward the light. The motors are on top of the car, in front of the rear wheels, and are held in place by a black plastic cover. Use the flat screwdriver to pry open the clip holding the cover on. The motors are shaped like little metal tubes. Gently remove the motors, being careful not to damage the wires. Swap the positions of the two motors. When the motors are in their new places, replace the cover. Test the new setup. The light sensor on one side should now control the wheel on the other side.

continues on next page . . .

4 Next, move the photoresistors to the top of the car. Carefully remove the three screws that hold the green circuit board onto the car. Turn the car over, and gently pry off the swivel wheel caster. A little cap will pop off on top of the circuit board. Save both pieces. Turn the car right side up again. Being very careful not to break any of the wires, wiggle the circuit board free. Keeping the wires attached to the car, tilt the board up. Turn it so the two light sensors are at the top of the board, facing forward. Build a cardboard support to keep the circuit board tilted up. Tape it in place.

5 The final step is to make a little wall between the sensors to keep the sensor on one side from detecting light coming from the other side. Again, you can just cut out a little square of cardboard and tape it between the sensors. Although it won't look fancy, you now have a bare-bones light-seeking robot. Test it out by placing it in a darkened spot. Move the beam of a flashlight near the robot and see if it will follow the light around.

MAKE A DIVIDER TO SEPARATE THE LIGHT SENSORS

CONTROLLERS: HOW ROBOTS THINK Chapter 6

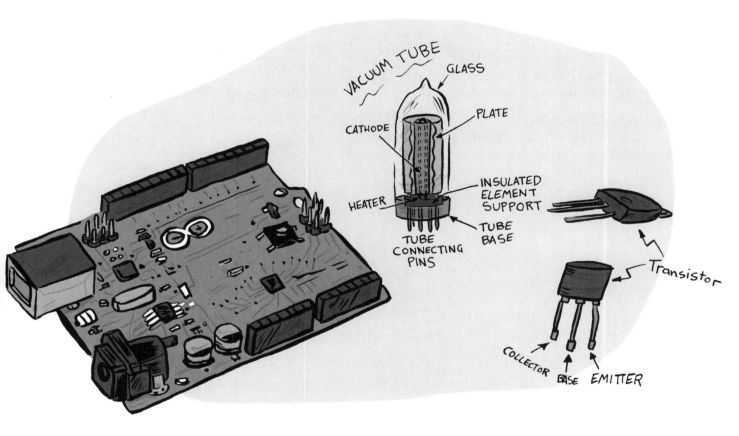

Even a simple vibrating or touch-sensor robot can move around in a lifelike way without anyone controlling it. But to make decisions on its own about what to do, a robot needs a brain.

Words to Know

vacuum tube: an electronic component that looks like a lightbulb. It was used as an on/off switch in early computers and other appliances.

transistor: an electronic component made of a solid piece of material and used as an on/off switch in electronic circuits.

silicon: a nonmetallic element found in clay and sand, used to make computer parts.

semiconductor: a material such as silicon that can vary the amount of electrical charge it will carry depending on certain conditions.

Early robots used **vacuum tubes**, a type of electronic switch that looked like a tall, thin lightbulb. Computers built with vacuum tubes were big enough to fill an entire room, and became very hot.

In 1947, the invention of the **transistor** made modern computers and robots possible. A transistor is a switch made from an element such as **silicon** that acts as a **semiconductor**. It is much easier to use than a vacuum tube, and much less breakable. Transistors can be used in combination with other components such as resistors and capacitors as the controller for simple robots.

Today, millions of transistors can be printed onto small squares of silicon known as computer chips, microprocessors, or integrated circuits (IC). Developed in 1958, microprocessors are the most important part of a computer. Yet they are so cheap and compact that they are found in almost every kind of electronic device, from cars to televisions. In a microprocessor, all the transistors and other components are miniaturized, wired together, and squeezed onto a flat thin square the size of your fingernail. With such a tiny distance to travel between components, electric currents can open and close the transistor "switches" incredibly fast.

As scientists figured out how to pack more computing power onto smaller and smaller chips, it became possible to give a robot its own computer. Most advanced robots now contain onboard computers. But scientists and hobbyists are constantly on the lookout for new technologies they can use to make their robots smarter, faster, and way more cool.

Words to Know

laptop: a small portable computer.

cloud computing: storing computer files or programs on the Internet instead of on your own computer.

Instead of designing and building a computer just for a robot, some experimental and hobby models use a standard **laptop** or tablet computer. Smartphones also make excellent robot controllers. Many smartphones not only have basic computing ability, but they also have their own camera, microphone, accelerometer, GPS, and other sensors.

One of the latest ideas in robotic control is *cloud computing*.

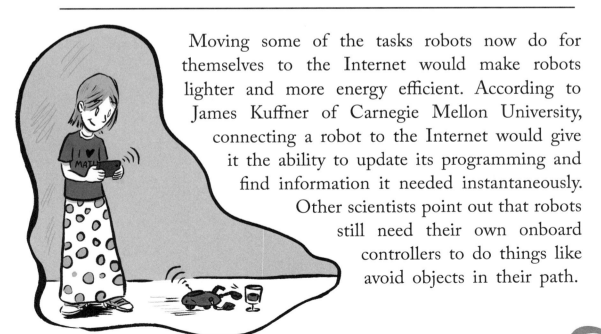

Moving some of the tasks robots now do for themselves to the Internet would make robots lighter and more energy efficient. According to James Kuffner of Carnegie Mellon University, connecting a robot to the Internet would give it the ability to update its programming and find information it needed instantaneously. Other scientists point out that robots still need their own onboard controllers to do things like avoid objects in their path.

Words to Know

memory: the part of a computer where information is stored.

For most robots built by kids or hobbyists, a microcontroller is the best choice. A microcontroller is a small, simple computer. They range from tinier than a postage stamp to the size of a playing card. Built into the microcontroller are a microprocessor, input/output devices, **memory**, and other parts. A microcontroller can be programmed like a regular computer, but it only has enough memory to hold a few instructions.

Even so, microcontrollers can be used to make robots behave in very complicated ways.

FUN FACTS

In 2008, researchers implanted a living "brain" grown from the cells of a rat into a robot and taught it to drive around objects. They created the cyborg to observe how the brain learns and how memories are formed.

Vacuum Tube Turtle Robots

A turtle robot is a small, simple robot used by students and researchers to learn about robot control. Low and round, or triangle-shaped with three or four wheels, they look like turtles as they roll slowly along the floor. In the 1940s, when computers were still new, a brain scientist in England named William Grey Walter built some of the earliest turtle robots using vacuum tubes. The robots were photovores that could "explore" their environment with light and touch sensors. Walter called them "tortoises," which is a kind of turtle, because they had shells that covered their electronic insides.

How a Computer Works—The Binary System

Every tiny electronic switch on a computer's microprocessor has only two settings: "on" or "off." If it's on, electricity is flowing through it. If it's off, no electricity flows through. When you program a computer, you are setting certain switches on or off. Since the computer deals with two choices, this method of making decisions is called the ***binary system***. ("Bi" comes from the Latin word for "two," as in bicycle and binoculars.) Mathematically, the two choices are represented by the numbers zero and one. If a switch is off, it is set to zero. If it is on, it is set to one. To a computer, a program looks like a long line of zeroes and ones.

Computer Programs

Computers are incredibly powerful. They are very good at solving simple problems that can be expressed mathematically, such as whether one number is bigger or smaller than another. They are also amazingly quick. They can solve billions of little problems each second. But by themselves they are not very smart. They need a human being to figure out how to take those little problems and put them together in useful ways.

Words to Know

binary system: a math system containing only zeroes and ones. It is used by computers to indicate whether a switch is on or off.

code or ***software:*** other names for a computer program.

So when a computer decides what a robot should do next based on a reading from a sensor, it's not really "thinking." It's taking the numbers produced by the sensor reading and comparing them to other numbers. It looks like the robot is making a decision, but it is really just carrying out a lot of little steps that a human being programmed into it. The directions for carrying out those steps is the computer program, also known as the computer ***code*** or ***software***. A person who writes computer code is called a programmer.

89

The most important part of writing a computer program is breaking down everything you want the computer to do into simple steps. Leave out a step, and the computer will get stuck, or do the wrong thing. One way to keep track of all the steps in a program is to start off by making a flowchart. Like the "Robot . . . or Not a Robot?" flowchart at the beginning of this book, it is a diagram with symbols for all the steps needed to complete a task.

Words to Know

conditional or **if-then-else statement:** a step in a program that gives a computer two choices depending on whether the answer to a certain test is yes or no.

Suppose you want to program a robot to follow a light. Your flowchart would have a decision block that says, "Is there light up ahead?" If the answer is "Yes," the program tells the robot to keep moving forward. If the answer is "No," it tells the robot to turn around. In the program, this will be shown as a statement that says, "If there is light ahead, then keep moving forward, or else turn around." This is called a **conditional** statement. Its outcome depends on whether or not a certain condition exists—in this case, whether or not there is light up ahead. It's also known as an **if-then-else statement**.

ACCORDING TO MY PROGRAMMING... IF IT'S WARM AND SUNNY...

THEN I SHOULD BUY ICE CREAM.

ROBOT

Conditional statements are an example of **Boolean logic**. Since a computer can only understand "on" and "off," every decision has to be boiled down to two choices. Logic is a way to turn every decision into a question with only two possible answers: "yes" or "no." These answers can then be translated into binary code: "on" or "off," one or zero. The most common logic operations that computer programs use are "NOT" (the condition is not true), "AND" (there are two conditions and both are true), and "OR" (there are two conditions and at least one of them is true).

Words to Know

Boolean logic: named after George Boole, it is a way to turn the decisions a computer makes into yes or no questions.

subroutine: a short piece of code that is given a name so it can be used multiple times in a program simply by inserting the name.

Even the most complicated computer programs can be written using these three logic operations and their variations!

Programmers can also use some shortcuts to keep from having to write the same steps over and over. They can write a **subroutine**, which is a small series of commands. Instead of writing out all the commands, the programmer can just write the name of the subroutine wherever those steps are needed. An example of a subroutine called "Blink" that tells a robot to move ahead 40 units and then flash its light for 5 seconds could look like this:

TO BLINK

forward 40

light on 5 seconds

light off

END

A **loop** repeats a command or series of commands as many times as you tell it to. For instance, if you wanted your robot to pick out all the green jelly beans from a bowl of mixed colors, you could write a loop like this: ············

In this example, the "WHILE" command tells the computer how to tell when it's time to stop. As long as there is at least one jelly bean in the bowl, the computer will keep going back to the beginning of the loop and doing it all over again. But when the number of jelly beans goes down to zero, the loop ends.

WHILE
the number of jelly beans in the bowl is 1 or more
Pick up 1 jelly bean
IF
jelly bean is green
THEN place it in the cup on the right
ELSE place it in a cup on the left.
END IF
END WHILE

Words to Know

loop: a short piece of code that is repeated a certain number of times until a specific condition is met.

Computer Languages

For humans, talking to other people is natural. But a computer thinks in binary code. That makes it hard for a computer to understand human language. So to communicate with a robot's brain, we use a special computer language. In fact, there are many different kinds of computer languages. Programmers can choose the language that is best suited for the job. Some popular computer languages in use today include C++, Java, and Python. These are used for everything from building web sites to animations to video games. They are also used to program robots.

```
1 int main ()
2 {
3   cout<< "Hello World!";
4   return 0;
5 }
```

NOW YOU'RE TALKING!

92

There are also simple programs designed for students and beginners. BASIC (which stands for Beginners' All-purpose Symbolic Instruction Code) is the first computer language many older adults learned. The codes used are similar to English, so they are easier to remember than more advanced computer languages. There are even a number of computer languages meant for kids. Some use very simple commands. Others are **graphical**.

Graphical languages use picture symbols instead of words. All you have to do is drag and drop the symbol on the computer screen. The symbols lock together like puzzle pieces, so you know that you have them in the right order. One of the earliest computer languages for kids was Logo. It was developed in 1967 by mathematician Seymour Papert of the MIT Artificial Intelligence Laboratory to program a turtle robot.

Early versions of the LEGO Mindstorms Robotics Invention System were programmed in Logo. Modern versions of Mindstorms use a more advanced program called LabView.

Words to Know

graphical: a programming language that lets users create programs by moving around small drawings or images on a computer screen.

bug: a mistake in a computer program.

debug: going through a computer program to find and remove any mistakes.

FUN FACTS

If your computer program doesn't work right, it probably has a **bug** in it. A bug is a mistake in the code. But in the old days vacuum tubes lit up the inside of computers like lightbulbs. And the light attracted moths. So every now and then, scientists would have to open up their computers and **debug** them. But instead of fixing a mistake in the code, they had to clean out the bodies of dead bugs!

How to Program in Logo

Today the computer language Logo is used to program realistic, on-screen virtual turtles as well as real robots. It uses simple commands to move the virtual turtle around the computer screen. The turtle is a cursor and as it moves, it draws a line that can be used to create designs. The commands let you tell the turtle to move forward or backward and how far to go. The number of spaces the turtle moves is measured in **pixels**. You can also tell it to turn right or left. The amount it turns is measured in degrees. A circle is divided into 360 degrees. To turn one quarter of the way around a circle, you go 90 degrees (¼ of 360 = 90). To turn halfway around so you are facing the opposite direction, you go 180 degrees (½ of 360 = 180). With just a few commands, you can get the virtual turtle to travel anywhere on the computer screen.

Words to Know

pixel: a tiny section of a digital image.

Here's a chart of some basic Logo commands. The letter "x" should be replaced with the number of spaces you want the turtle to move. The letter "y" is where you put the number of degrees you want the turtle robot to turn. "Pen Up" tells the turtle robot to stop drawing as it moves. "Pen Down" tells it to start drawing again.

Command	Meaning
FD x	Go Forward x pixels
BK x	Go Back x pixels
RT y	Turn Right y degrees
LT y	Turn Left y degrees
PU	Pen Up
PD	Pen Down
REPEAT n [XX x YY y]	Repeat the commands shown in the brackets. (That is how a loop is done in Logo.) You can have any number of commands, in any order.
	n = the number of times the loop is repeated
	XX = a command to move (FD or BK)
	YY = a command to turn (RT or LT)

WRITE A PEN-AND-PAPER LOGO PROGRAM (#1)

Computer programmers usually write out their programs before testing them on the computer. But you can test a Logo program without a computer! Just pretend that you are the turtle robot and follow the commands in the program. Instead of a computer screen, you will be drawing on a piece of graph paper. If you want to try it on a computer, download a copy of Logo onto your computer and type in your finished program to see how it runs! (You can find the links at the end of this chapter.)

1 Turn the paper sideways, so it is wider than it is high. Each box on the graph paper will count as 10 pixels. That will make it come out about the same size as on a computer screen.

2 To start, place your pen 10 boxes down from the top and five boxes in from the left. Make a mark on your starting place. Always start with the turtle pointing up! Since the Logo turtle usually looks like a triangle on the screen, you can make a mark like a little triangle pointing up to remind you which way to go.

3 Follow the commands as if your pen was the Logo turtle. You can have a friend read the commands to you.

4 To draw a square, you have to tell the turtle to draw four lines, turning at the corners each time.

FD 60 RT 90, FD 60 RT 90
FD 60 RT 90, FD 60 RT 90

A shorter way to write the same program is to use a loop:

REPEAT 4 [FD 60 RT 90]

Try following either of these programs to see how a virtual turtle uses commands to draw a square!

```
FD 60 RT 90
FD 60 RT 90
FD 60 RT 90
FD 60 RT 90
      OR
REPEAT 4 [FD 60 RT 90]
```

SUPPLIES

- several sheets of graph paper
- pencils
- several sheets of lined paper
- a friend (optional)

WRITE A PEN-AND-PAPER LOGO PROGRAM (#2)

Now that you know how to simulate a turtle robot with a pencil and paper, try carrying out a subroutine. In Logo, a subroutine is called a "procedure." No matter what you call it, it is a short program that you name so it can be used over and over. When you type the name of the subroutine into Logo, it carries out all the commands in the subroutine.

The subroutine in this activity will draw a square like before. But this square can also be used as a simple letter "O" in a word. Since we make letters by starting at the left and going to the right, this subroutine will finish the square by moving the turtle to the right of the letter.

1 The first step is to give the subroutine a name—in this case, "ostrich." Then we tell Logo how to carry out the subroutine "ostrich" with the command "TO" like this:

SUPPLIES

- several sheets of graph paper
- several sheets of lined paper
- pencils
- a friend (optional)

```
TO ostrich
REPEAT 4 [FD 60 RT 90]
        RT 90
        FD 60
        END
```

Notice the "END" at the bottom. Leaving out an "END" code can cause a lot of problems, so don't forget it when you're programming!

2 Find a clean space on the graph paper and draw a little triangle pointing up with the pencil to mark your starting point, as before. Then follow the subroutine "ostrich" with your pencil and see if you end up with an "O."

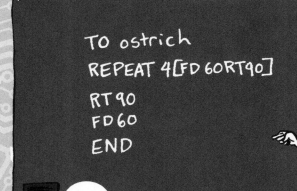

```
TO ostrich
REPEAT 4 [FD 60 RT 90]
RT 90
FD 60
END
```

3 Practice with a subroutine "rhino" which draws a letter "R" and "deer" which draws a letter "D."

TO rhino	TO deer
FD 60	FD 60
RT 90	RT 90
FD 30	FD 30
RT 90	RT 90
FD 30	FD 60
RT 90	RT 90
FD 30	FD 30
BK 40	RT 180
LT 90	FD 30
FD 30	END
LT 90	
END	

4 Once you've got the hang of it, try writing a subroutine of your own to make a space between one letter and the next in a word. Remember "PU" means move ahead without drawing and "PO" means pen down! The subroutine will have to include these steps:

• Get ready to move without drawing.

• Move ahead 30 pixels.

• Point the turtle up (so it's ready for the start of the next letter in the word).

• Get ready to start drawing again.

The routine should be called "snake." (If you have trouble, take a peek at page 99.)

5 Now, using the subroutines for the letters and spaces you have learned, try writing a program that uses them to spell a word. For instance, you can create a subroutine called "rod" like this:

TO rod
rhino
ostrich
deer
END

If you want, create a subroutine to make the turtle write several words on one line using the snake subroutine to separate them. For instance, you can write a subroutine called "phrase" to spell out the phrase "door or rod" by using a subroutine for each word. You can keep **nesting** subroutines. When you're done, test out your programs on your graph paper or Logo program and see how they work!

> ### Words to Know
>
> **nesting:** a way of organizing a computer program so that one subroutine contains other subroutines.

WRITE A PEN-AND-PAPER LOGO PROGRAM (#3)

Using subroutines, we can program a pencil/turtle in Logo to write out an entire sentence! Usually, the first thing students learn in any new computer language is a program that writes out the words "Hello World." Most languages come with a "Hello World" program built in, but we can write our own in Logo. It's not hard, but it will take some time and patience. You already know how to write a subroutine that will draw an "O" and make spaces between letters. Now you will have to figure out subroutines to write the rest of the letters. Here's how to get started:

SUPPLIES

- several sheets of graph paper
- pencils
- several sheets of lined paper
- a friend (optional)

1 All the letters in "HELLO WORLD" can be formed out of simple shapes that will be easy to program in Logo. (See the illustration.) Here are names for all the subroutines you will need:

> hippo = H
> elephant = E
> lion = L
> ostrich = O
> warthog = W
> rhino = R
> deer = D
> snake =
> space between letters (30 pixels)
> spider =
> space between words (60 pixels)

2 Write subroutines for all the letters. (You already have programs for "O," "R," and "D.") Test them out before moving on to the next step.

3 Write a subroutine called "hello" to spell out "HELLO WORLD" using the subroutines for the letters and spaces. When you're done, test it out on your graph paper. If you run out of room, tape a second sheet onto the first, lining up all the boxes. (If you need help, take a peek at the answers on the next two pages.)

4 Extra credit: Can you come up with a subroutine to draw an exclamation point? If so, add it at the end!

Answers to Logo Programming

TO hello	TO snake	TO spider
hippo	PU	PU
snake	FD 30	FD 60
elephant	PD	PD
snake	LT 90	LT 90
REPEAT 2 [lion snake]	END	END
ostrich		
spider		
warthog		
snake		
ostrich		
snake		
rhino		
snake		
lion		
snake		
deer		
snake		
END		

continues on next page . . .

TO hippo	TO elephant	TO lion	TO ostrich	TO warthog	TO rhino	TO deer
FD 60	FD 60	FD 60	REPEAT 4 [FD 60 RT 90]	FD 60	FD 60	FD 60
BK 30	RT 90	BK 60	RT 90	BK 60	RT 90	RT 90
RT 90	FD 60	RT 90	FD 60	RT 90	FD 30	FD 30
FD 60	RT 90	FD 60	END	FD 30	RT 90	RT 90
LT 90	PU	END		LT 90	FD 30	FD 60
FD 30	FD 30			FD 60	RT 90	RT 90
BK 60	RT 90			BK 60	FD 30	FD 30
RT 90	PD			RT 90	BK 40	RT 180
END	FD 60			FD 30	LT 90	FD 30
	LT 90			LT 90	FD 30	END
	FD 30			FD 60	LT 90	
	LT 90			BK 60	END	
	FD 60			RT 90		
	END			END		

BINARY BEAD JEWELRY

Using only two colors of beads, you can write a message in binary code. Since computers can only detect zeroes and ones, a code called ASCII (which stands for American Standard Code for Information Interchange) was invented to translate letters and numbers to binary form. Computers read each zero or one (also known as a "binary digit," or **bit**) in groups of eight (known as a **byte**), so there are eight digits in each ASCII code.

To make each binary bead letter, you'll be sliding eight beads onto a paper clip. You can pick any two colors to represent zero and one. Then decide what you want to write. You'll need about eight paperclips to make a bracelet, more for a necklace!

SUPPLIES
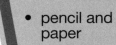

- pencil and paper
- medium-size beads in two colors
- paper plate
- 8 paper clips (more for a necklace)
- glue

Words to Know

bit: the basic unit of information storage in a computer, consisting of a zero or one.

byte: a group of eight bits that is treated as a single piece of information.

ASCII Characters	
Letter	Binary Code
A	01000001
B	01000010
C	01000011
D	01000100
E	01000101
F	01000110
G	01000111
H	01001000
I	01001001
J	01001010
K	01001011
L	01001100
M	01001101
N	01001110
O	01001111
P	01010000
Q	01010001
R	01010010
S	01010011
T	01010100
U	01010101
V	01010110
W	01010111
X	01011000
Y	01011001
Z	01011010
space	00100000

continues on next page . . .

YOU NEED:
GLUE
×8
TWO COLORS OF BEADS
PAPER PLATE

1 Decide on a message that can fit on a bracelet or necklace. Draw two columns on a piece of paper. In the first column, write your message out, putting each letter on its own row. In the second column, use the chart to write in the ASCII binary code for each letter. (For numbers and other symbols, find an ASCII character chart online.) Here's what your columns would look like if you wanted to spell out the word "ROBOT":

R	01010010
O	01001111
B	01000010
O	01001111
T	01010100

2 Pick one color bead for "zero" and another for "one." Pour a few beads of each color on a paper plate. Take the first paper clip and bend open the end slightly. Use the end of the paperclip to pick up each bead. Look at the code you have written out to guide you. For instance, for the letter "R," if you are using white for zero and black for one, you would slide on the beads in this order: white, black, white, black, white, white, black, white. Add a dab of glue to the first and last beads to hold them in place on the paperclip. Lay the paperclip down in front of you so you can read your binary code letter going left to right.

Words to Know

open source: a computer program or electronic device whose design can be used, copied, or modified by the public for free.

download: to copy computer files from the Internet to your own computer.

3 Do the same with the next paperclip letter. Then, turning it to face the same way as the first one, hook the second paperclip onto the first. Continue with the rest of the letters in your message. Then just hook the last paperclip onto the first and you're done!

THANKS! NOW I CAN MAKE ONE WITH YOUR NAME.

Program a Robot on Your Computer

On the Internet you can find many **open source** computer languages that kids can use for free. Some can be used online. Others have to be **downloaded** to your computer. Here are a few that can be used to program robots, along with web sites that help you learn how to use them:

- **Logo** (there are lots of variations—here are some good ones for kids)
  - http://www.mathsnet.net/Logo/turtleLogo/index.html
  - http://fmslogo.sourceforge.net/
  - http://el.media.mit.edu/logo-foundation
- **Scratch** (can be used with the LEGO Education WeDo Robotics Kit for 7–12 year olds)
  - http://scratch.mit.edu/
  - http://wiki.scratch.mit.edu/wiki/LEGO_Education_WeDo_Robotics_Kit
- **RoboMind** (a simple and fun virtual robot with nice-looking graphics)
  - http://www.robomind.net/en/index.html

| # AI, SOCIAL ROBOTS, AND THE FUTURE OF ROBOTICS

It's one thing to program a robot to "think." But getting it to think like a human? That's a goal scientists have been working on since computers were developed. And they're not quite there yet, but getting closer every day.

It's true that computers can solve number problems faster and more accurately than even the greatest math whiz. But when it comes to making decisions and figuring out what to do in a new situation, people still have computers beat. The science of Artificial Intelligence (AI) is all about figuring out how to make computer brains smarter, so they don't need people to tell them what to do.

One approach scientists have tried is to program computers to act human, even if they don't really think the same way we do. In 1966, Joseph Weizenbaum of MIT designed Eliza, a computer program that behaved like a counselor. A person could "talk" to Eliza by typing in a sentence on a keyboard and reading the response on a computer screen.

Words to Know

chatbot: an AI program designed to have natural-sounding conversations with humans.

The program started every conversation by saying, "Hi, I'm Eliza. What's your problem?" When you typed in an answer, she would respond with a related sentence, such as, "Tell me more." Although it was a very simple program, Eliza seemed to pass the Turing test. People talked to it as if it were a real person. Today these kinds of programs are called **chatbots**. When you make a phone call to a company or school and a computer voice asks you questions to find out who you are looking for, you are talking to a chatbot!

How to Tell If You're Human

If you have ever gone to a web site that asks you to sign in by copying a series of weird-looking letters, you've taken a CAPTCHA test. Developed by scientists at Carnegie Mellon University, it stands for "Completely Automated Public Turing test to tell Computers and Humans Apart." The letters on a CAPTCHA test are supposed to be too distorted for a computer to read. It's really a reverse Turing test to make sure you're not a robot!

Challenging a computer to a game is another way to test how smart it really is. In 1989, World Chess Champion Garry Kasparov played two games against an IBM computer called Deep Thought. Kasparov defeated the computer both times. But in 1997, an improved version called Deep Blue played against Kasparov and won!

As it turned out, chess is a game that's easy for computers to master. All they have to do is memorize every possible move the pieces can make. Then they check all the possibilities to see which is most likely to lead to a victory. Modern computers can do these kinds of calculations in the blink of an eye.

It's much harder to teach a computer to play a TV game show like Jeopardy.

In 2011, people across the country watched as an IBM computer named Watson beat two top human players. Jeopardy is a game in which players are given an answer and have to guess the question that goes with it. To win, players must know about a wide range of subjects. But researcher David Ferrucci and his team had to do more than fill Watson's memory banks with information. They had to teach Watson how to understand the clues, which often contain tricky wording and jokes.

All-time Jeopardy champion Ken Jennings was one of the players who lost to the computer. In the final round when he didn't know the answer, Jennings saluted Watson's ability by writing, "I for one welcome our new computer overlords."

One reason Watson won Jeopardy was that it got better at playing as it went along. It was able to learn by watching what the other players were doing. Designing programs that can "learn how to learn" is another goal of Artificial Intelligence researchers. Simon is a humanoid robot developed by roboticist Andrea Thomaz of the Georgia Institute of Technology in 2009. It learns by figuring out what people are doing and copying them. For instance, Simon can watch someone sort toys into different bins. By observing, it can figure out if they are sorting them by color or shape and then do the job itself. Simon can also ask questions and get people to explain things to it. With a doll-like white plastic face and glowing oval ears, Simon uses its cute looks to get people to help it learn.

Words to Know

app: short for "application," a program that runs on a phone, tablet, or other computerized device.

Social robots

Even thinking like a human isn't enough for some scientists. They'd like to develop robots with personalities! A social robot can be friendly, and even lovable. Many researchers believe that robots that show feelings are easier for human beings to work with.

FUN FACTS

Siri, a mobile phone *app*, is a chatbot that can learn. It responds to spoken questions and commands. Siri can read text messages out loud, place calls, order tickets or shop online, tell you what the weather is like, or find stores and addresses. The more you use Siri, the more information it gathers about you. That helps it decide what you like and what kind of suggestions you are looking for.

107

In 1998, Cynthia Breazeal of the MIT Media Lab Personal Robots Group produced Kismet. This robotic face has cow-like ears, rubbery lips, and large eyes. When you talk to Kismet, its expression changes from happy to sad to surprised, depending on your tone of voice. Other social robots from Breazeal's lab include Leonardo, a fuzzy-faced robot designed by Hollywood special effects expert Stan Winston.

Nexi, built in 2008, is a mobile robot with a Segway-like rolling body and humanoid hands. Nexi can shrug its shoulders to show puzzlement and raise its eyebrows to show surprise. In 2009, Breazeal's team set up Nexi at a robotics exhibit at the Museum of Science in Boston, Massachusetts, to study the way visitors interact with social robots.

One use for social robots may be as companions for older people and children.

In 2008, a study by Saint Louis University found that a robotic dog called Aibo was just as good at cheering people up as a live dog. In the experiment, a mutt named Sparky visited some residents at a home for the elderly. Others spent time with Aibo. Although Aibo looked like a toy, it could play with a ball, wag its tail, and roll over.

Aibo's cameras and distance-finding sensors let it respond to people and objects around it. Aibo's programming was so lifelike that it would sometimes disobey orders!

The scientists reported that robots can make good pets for people who are not able to take care of real animals.

Another robotic pet, a baby seal named Paro, is specially designed for nursing homes. Developed by Japanese engineer Takanori Shibata, the furry robot helps patients relax when they are worried. Paro has touch, light, sound, and temperature sensors that tell it how it is being held. It can also recognize some words and make sounds like a real baby harp seal. Paro is programmed to respond happily to praise and cuddling. Shibata has said he chose to make Paro look like a seal because most people have never seen a real seal up close. He believes patients are more accepting of a robotic seal than of a dog or cat.

In 2004, scientists began testing a robot named Rubi in a preschool class. Roboticist Javier Movellan of the University of California in San Diego designed the friendly teacher bot because his research robots looked scary to toddlers in the day care center. Rubi looks something like a TV set with a head, arms, and clothes. A touchscreen on its tummy lets kids interact with it. Toddlers loved Rubi so much it became a problem. On its first day in class, two boys pulled the robot's arms off! After that, the designers programmed Rubi to cry if a child got too rough. Tests have shown that the robot can help young kids learn new words.

109

Scientists are also using social robots to help autistic children who have trouble playing and talking with other people. Roboticists Hideki Kozima and Marek Michalowski developed a little dancing robot named Keepon that could draw the attention of autistic children with its bouncy movements. The robot, which is small enough to sit on a desk, looks like a tiny yellow snowman. Its eyes and nose are just black dots. But it can nod, turn, tilt, and bob up and down to show that it's happy or sad.

In 2007, Keepon made a music video that became a hit on the Internet and won fans around the world. So in 2011, the scientists released a toy version called My Keepon. Like the original, My Keepon's microphone lets it match the beat of the music. Through touch sensors under its soft rubbery skin, it reacts to poking, patting, and squeezing by looking around and making sounds.

A Robot that Makes Humans Friendlier

In 2008, New York artist Kacie Kinzer set a cute cardboard "robot" called a Tweenbot loose in a city park to see how people would react. The Tweenbot could only roll forward in a straight line. It carried a sign that asked for help to get it to the other side of the park. Many people stopped to turn the robot in the right direction or fix it when it got stuck. One person gave it a ride across the park on his bike. A few even tried telling it where to go—even though it was just a cardboard box with a motor and a drawn-on face. Kinzer has said people automatically smiled when they saw Tweenbot's smiling face. She calls her social robot project a way to make humans act more like humans.

Some of the money from the sale of My Keepon will go to the development of more Keepon research robots to help kids with autism.

Robots versus Humans?

Is it wrong to use robots as pets and companions? That's the kind of question Sherry Turkle of MIT would like people to ask themselves. Turkle studies how technology affects people's lives. She thinks robots that do boring chores for people are great. But she wonders about the **ethics** of letting robots babysit for children or take care of the elderly or disabled.

Social robots act friendly, but they are only doing what they are programmed to do. Turkle has worked with children who thought a broken robot had stopped liking them. Do you think a robot companion with a faulty program could hurt someone's feelings? These are questions that may become more important as robots become a bigger part of our lives.

People have long wondered whether robots are helpful or harmful. In *I, Robot*, author Isaac Asimov created three Laws of Robotics. The laws were designed to make sure that robots would not be able to harm humans.

Words to Know

ethics: whether something is right or wrong.

111

- **Law 1:** A robot may not injure a human being or, through inaction, allow a human being to come to harm.

- **Law 2:** A robot must obey orders given to it by human beings, except where such orders would conflict with the First Law.

- **Law 3:** A robot must protect its own existence as long as such protection does not conflict with the First or Second Law.

- **A fourth law was later added:** A robot may not injure humanity or, through inaction, allow humanity to come to harm. As it turns out, Asimov's Laws have not been followed in real life. Robots are often used to fight wars and terrorism.

Should people be worried about robots?

In movies like *The Terminator*, robots rebel against their human creators and try to take over the world. In reality, such a takeover is unlikely. Scientists are still a long way from creating robots that can function completely on their own. And most robots are designed to help humans, not harm them. Roboticist Daniel H. Wilson, author of *How to Survive a Robot Uprising* and *A Boy and His Bot*, has a message for kids: "We have nothing to fear from robots—they can be powerful tools and good friends. But if you notice that a robot has glowing red eyes, be sure to stay away from its pincers!"

So You Want to Build Robots . . .

Building and programming robots is a great hobby for kids. And kids can learn a lot from it, too. In Georgia, students used LEGO Mindstorms kits to create all kinds of exciting projects. One year they created a lunar landscape in a closet to simulate a robot exploration mission. They built the rugged surface out of crushed gravel and poured concrete. They also designed a lander that was lowered from the ceiling. To make their project even more realistic, they set up a video to show them what the robot was doing. The video had a delay of several seconds, the time it takes for a signal to travel from the moon to Earth. Another class put together a robot chef competition, where the contestants had to gather ingredients to make a balanced meal.

The robots inspired students to learn new things they never would have tried before.

RobotGrrl Erin Kennedy thinks kids shouldn't worry that robotics is hard. "They don't need to know anything specific at the start, which is the best part," she says. "As they learn more about robotics, they'll be able to apply their problem-solving skills to conquer different challenges. The best skill to have is patience, and the character to never give up."

DESIGN A SOCIAL ROBOT EXPERIMENT

The Tweenbot was an art project, not a scientific experiment. But many scientists believe that the best way to study how people react to robots is "in the wild." That means seeing what people do with robots in an everyday setting. In a laboratory, the scientists can control what goes on. Out in the real world, anything can happen! People may ignore the robot, or accidentally break it, like the preschoolers who tore off Rubi's arm. Or they may start to play or talk with it in unexpected ways. These observations can help roboticists design friendlier, more useful robots.

You can design your own Tweenbot-type experiment to find out how people interact with a robot under normal circumstances. If there is something you'd like to get people to do, make a **hypothesis** about how a robot can encourage them to do it. Then test your hypothesis by gathering data. (In this case, "data" means measurements or facts that can be compared, such as how many people stopped to interact with your robot as opposed to how many passed it by.) Collect data by watching what people do around your robot. Take notes, photos, or videos as a record of what you see. Or ask people what they saw and felt afterward in a face-to-face interview or on a written survey. Then look over your data and decide whether your hypothesis was correct.

I WONDER IF PEOPLE WOULD CALL THEIR MOMS WHEN THEY SEE IT.

Words to Know

hypothesis: a guess about how or why something works that can be tested with experiments to see if it is true.

WHAT A GREAT IDEA!

You can build a simple sign-carrying robot that asks people for help, like the Tweenbot. One early version didn't even move, but sat on a shelf or wall for people passing by to find. Or you can build a more complicated robot. One example might be to test whether a robotic recycling bin could encourage people to recycle their drink containers by flashing lights or playing music when someone puts a bottle in it.

A social robot experiment might make a good project for a science fair. And who knows, your results might even help scientists create better social robots!

CALL YOUR MOM SHE'D LOVE IT :)

How to Get Started

If the simple robot projects in this book make you want to try more, you're in luck! There are many ways to get started in robotics. See if there's a robotics team in your school or area. Many colleges offer summer and weekend robotics camps and workshops for kids. And youth organizations like the Boy Scouts and 4-H are adding robotics to their programs. Of course, you can always create robots on your own using kits or DIY projects in books and online. Here are some kits and competitions kids can try. You'll find more robotics resources for beginners in the back of the book. Have fun seeing what kind of robots you can come up with!

- **LEGO Mindstorms,** http://mindstorms.lego.com
- **VEX Robotics,** http://www.vexrobotics.com
- **ProtoSnap MiniBot Kit,** http://www.sparkfun.com
- **LittleBits,** http://littlebits.cc
- **First LEGO League,** http://www.firstlegoleague.org/
- **Botball,** http://www.botball.org/

GLOSSARY

accelerometer: an electronic device that measures acceleration.

actuator: a piece of equipment that makes a robot move.

alternating current (AC): electricity that flows back and forth at a steady rate.

amputee: a person who is missing an arm or leg.

animatronic: making a puppet or other lifelike figure move on its own with electronics.

app: short for "application," a program that runs on a phone, tablet, or other computerized device.

assembly line: a way of putting together products in a factory by passing materials from one machine or person to another to do the next step.

atoms: the extremely tiny building blocks that make up all chemicals.

automata: machines that can move by themselves (singular is automaton).

autonomous: a robot that can plan its movements and move without human help.

battery: a device that produces electricity using chemicals.

BEAM: a type of simple, solar-powered, lifelike robot controlled by a simple circuit.

binary system: a math system containing only zeroes and ones. It is used by computers to indicate whether a switch is on or off.

biomimetic: a machine or material that copies a living thing.

bionic: a mechanical or computer-driven device that replaces or improves the normal ability of a body part.

bit: the basic unit of information storage in a computer, consisting of a zero or one.

Boolean logic: named after George Boole, it is a way to turn the decisions a computer makes into yes or no questions.

bug: a mistake in a computer program.

byte: a group of eight bits that is treated as a single piece of information.

capacitor: an electrical component (like a battery) that stores an electrical charge and releases it all at once when needed.

caster: a wheel or ball-shaped roller that can swivel to point in any direction.

chatbot: an AI program designed to have natural-sounding conversations with humans.

chemical: the pure form of a substance. Some chemicals can be combined or broken up to create new chemicals.

circuit: a path that lets electricity flow when closed in a loop.

clean room: a room in a laboratory or factory where objects that must be kept free of dust or dirt are made.

cloud computing: storing computer files or programs on the Internet instead of on your own computer.

cochlear implant: an electronic device that is attached to nerves under the skin to help a deaf person detect sounds.

code: another name for a computer program.

communication: sharing information with another person or machine.

computer: a device for storing and working with information.

computer program: a set of step-by-step instructions that tells a computer what to do with the information it has to work with.

conditional: a step in a program that gives a computer two choices depending on whether the answer to a certain test is yes or no.

controller: a switch, computer, or microcontroller that can react to what the sensor detects.

cyborg: a human or animal that is part robot.

data: information, usually given in the form of numbers, that can be processed by a computer.

debug: going through a computer program to find and remove any mistakes.

degrees of freedom: the number of directions in which a robotic effector or other part can move.

direct current (DC): electricity that flows in one direction.

DIY: do-it-yourself.

download: to copy computer files from the Internet to your own computer.

drive system: wheels, legs, or other parts that make a robot move.

echo: sound waves that bounce off a distant object and reflect back to the place they started.

effector: a device that lets the robot affect things in the outside world, such as a gripper, tool, laser beam, or display panel.

electricity: a form of energy released when electrons are in motion.

electromagnet: a temporary magnet created by running electricity through a magnet.

electron: a part of an atom that has a negative charge. It can move from one atom to another.

electronics: devices that use computer parts to control the flow of electricity.

emitter: a device that emits, or sends out, a light or sound wave or other signal.

engineering: the use of science and math in the design and construction of things.

ethics: whether something is right or wrong.

evolve: a change in a species of living thing in response to the world around it.

feedback: information about the result of an action that is sent back to the person or machine that performed the action.

flowchart: a diagram that shows the steps to go through to solve a problem.

force: a push or pull that changes the speed or direction of an object.

gears: wheels with interlocking teeth that transfer motion from one part of a machine to another.

GPS: Global Positioning System, a device that determines its location on Earth using signals sent from different satellites in space.

graphical: a programming language that lets users create programs by moving around small drawings or images on a computer screen.

hacking: using electronics skills to make a device do something it was not designed to do.

humanoid: looking like a human being.

hydraulic: a system that pushes and pulls objects using tubes filled with fluid.

hypothesis: a guess about how or why something works that can be tested with experiments to see if it is true.

if-then-else statement: a step in a program that gives a computer two choices depending on whether the answer to a certain test is yes or no.

industrial: used in a factory, or designed to be used under hard work conditions.

infrared (IR): a type of light with a longer wavelength than visible light, which can also be felt as heat.

input: a signal or information that is put into a machine or electrical system.

Internet: a communications network that allows computers around the world to share information.

joint: a place on a robot arm or other part where it can bend or turn.

laptop: a small portable computer.

lever: a bar or handle used to run or adjust something.

lidar: a device that measures distance by shining light at an object and measuring the time it takes for the light to reflect back.

line-following: a robot that uses sensors to detect and follow a line on the ground.

loom: a machine for weaving thread into cloth.

loop: a short piece of code that is repeated a certain number of times until a specific condition is met.

memory: the part of a computer where information is stored.

microcontroller: a very small device that works like a mini-computer.

microscopic: something so small it can only be seen using a microscope.

modular: robots that can work alone or be connected in different combinations to form a larger robot.

nesting: a way of organizing a computer program so that one subroutine contains other subroutines.

non-Newtonian fluid: a substance that can hold its shape like a solid and flow like a liquid.

nuclear: energy produced when the nucleus of an atom is split apart.

nucleus: the center of an atom.

open source: a computer program or electronic device whose design can be used, copied, or modified by the public for free.

output: the movement or other response of a robot to the input it receives from its sensors.

passive dynamic: a robot walker that is powered by gravity.

photoresistor: a light sensor that works by changing the resistance in an electrical current depending on the amount of light.

photovore: a robot that chases light.

pixel: a tiny section of a digital image.

plasma torch: a tool that uses streams of electrified gas to cut through sheets of metal.

pneumatic: a system that pushes and pulls objects using tubes filled with air or other gases.

portable: easily moved around.

powered exoskeleton: a "robot suit" that can be worn to give a person added strength.

prototype: an experimental model.

punch card: a card with holes punched in it that gives directions to a machine or computer.

radar: a device that detects objects by bouncing microwaves or radio waves off them and measuring how long it takes for the waves to return.

radioactive: a substance made of atoms that gives off nuclear energy.

radio transmitter: the part of a radio that sends signals.

repel: to push away.

robot: a machine that is able to sense, think, and act on its own.

roboticist: a scientist who works with robots.

robotics: the science of designing, building, controlling, and operating robots.

scavenged: saved from something that is broken or no longer used.

science fiction: a story set in the future about contact with other worlds and imaginary science and technology.

semiconductor: a material such as silicon that can vary the amount of electrical charge it will carry depending on certain conditions.

Sense-Think-Act Cycle: a decision-making process used by robots.

sensor: in robotics, a device to detect what's going on outside the machine.

servo: a motor that can be can be controlled electronically.

silicon: a nonmetallic element found in clay and sand, used to make computer parts.

smart home: a house in which all electric devices are monitored or controlled by a computer.

smartphone: a mobile phone that can also be used like a simple computer to play games, send email, watch movies, etc.

social robot: a robot designed to talk, play, or work with humans in a lifelike way.

software: another name for a computer program.

solar cell: a device that converts the energy in light into electrical energy.

solenoid: an electromagnetic device that pushes a rod up and down.

sonar: a way to detect objects by bouncing sound waves off them and measuring how long it takes to detect an echo.

stability: how well something can stay in its proper position.

subroutine: a short piece of code that is given a name so it can be used multiple times in a program simply by inserting the name.

swarm: a group of identical robots designed to work together as a team.

switch: a device that controls the flow of electricity through a circuit.

syringe: a medical instrument used to inject fluid into the body or take fluid out.

tablet: a small, flat portable computer with a touchscreen instead of a keyboard for entering information.

technology: scientific or mechanical tools and methods used to do something.

telepresence: a robotic device that uses video and other types of sensors and displays to let someone in one place act and feel like they are in a room someplace else.

terminal: the point on a battery where electricity flows in or out.

theremin: an electronic musical instrument that plays different notes when you move your hands around it without touching it.

torque: the amount of force it takes to make something turn or spin.

transistor: an electronic component made of a solid piece of material and used as an on/off switch in electronic circuits.

Turing test: a series of questions to test whether a computer can think like a human being.

ultraviolet (UV): a type of light with a shorter wavelength than visible light, also called black light.

Uncanny Valley: the point at which a robot looks almost real and becomes strange and frightening.

Unmanned Aerial Vehicles (UAVs): planes and other aircraft that can fly without a pilot in control.

vacuum tube: an electronic component that looks like a lightbulb. It was used as an on/off switch in early computers and other appliances.

vibrobot: a robot-like toy that moves using a vibrating motor.

webcam: a camera attached to a computer that can send photos or video over the Internet.

weld: to connect metal parts by heating them until they soften.

RESOURCES

Information About Robots

- *How to Survive a Robot Uprising.*
  Daniel H. Wilson. Bloomsbury Publishing, 2005.
- *How to Build a Robot Army.*
  Daniel H. Wilson. Bloomsbury Publishing, 2007.
- *Robots: From Everyday to Out of this World.*
  Editors of YES Mag, Kids Can Press, 2008.
- *Robots in Science and Medicine.*
  Steve Parker. Amicus, 2011.
- *Robots for Work and Fun.*
  Steve Parker. Amicus, 2011.
- *SCRATCHbot.*
  Adam Woog. Nowood House Press, 2011.
- *The Nexi Robot.*
  Toney Allman, Norwood House Press, 2010.
- *Robotics.*
  Helena Domaine. Lerner Publications, 2006.
- *Ultimate Robot.* Robert Malone. DK, 2004.

Robot Building

- *How to Build Your Own Prize-Winning Robot.*
  Ed Sobey. Enslow Publishers, 2002.
- *Robot Invasion: 7 Cool and Easy Robot Projects.*
  Dave Johnson. McGraw-Hill/OsborneMedia, 2002.
- *The LEGO Mindstorms NXT 2.0 Discovery Book:
  A Beginner's Guide to Building and
  Programming Robots.* Laurens Valk. No Starch
  Press, 2010.
- *Robot Builder's Bonanza (Fourth Edition).*
  Gordon McComb. McGraw Hill, 2011.
- *Robot Building for Beginners (Second Edition).*
  David Cook. Apress, 2009.
- *Unscrewed: Salvage and Reuse Motors, Gears,
  Switches, and More from Your Old Electronics.*
  Ed Sobey. Chicago Review Press, 2011.
- *Make: Electronics (Learn by Discovery).*
  Charles Platt. Make, 2009.

Kits and Supplies

- *SparkFun* (sparkfun.com): Electronics and robotics
  kits and parts for beginners and experts.
- *Solarbotics* (solarbotics.com): Kits, parts, and
  books for simple BEAM and other types of robots.

Web Sites

- *Instructables: Simple Bots*
  How-tos for building battery-powered robots from
  scratch. **www.instructables.com/id/Simple-Bots/**
- *The Robotics Alliance Project*
  NASA's robotics website for students and the
  public. **www.robotics.nasa.gov**
- *Society of Robots*
  Lots of robot-building tutorials and a forum to ask
  questions. **www.societyofrobots.com**
- *Robot Magazine*
  News about student, hobby and consumer robots
  for general readers. **www.botmag.com**
- *Make: Projects "Guide to Robotics"*
  Lots of helpful info from Make Magazine (sponsors of
  Maker Faire). **www.makeprojects.com/c/Robotics**
- *Let's Make Robots*
  Another site for hobbyists to share photos, tutorials,
  etc. **www.letsmakerobots.com**
- *TEDTalks*
  Videos of fascinating short talks
  by inventors, scientists, and other
  thinkers. **www.ted.com**

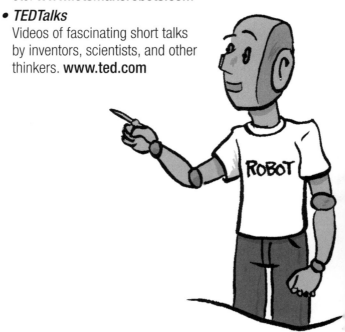